ACKNOWL.

C000205405

For Val, Laurie and Chris

Many thanks to a true gentleman of the profession; Jimmy Perry OBE, for his kind words of endorsement. Thanks also to Terry Denton de Gray and his World of Fantasy for supplying the costume for the cover photograph, and my old chums Brian Ward and Ian Durrant for their help and inspiration. A special big thank you goes to Richard and David Cockerill of Arlon House Publishing for having faith in this project.

And finally, to all the agents who for months on end gave me no work ... thanks for nothing!

. . . .

First published in Great Britain (1997)
by Arlon House Publishing
Printed and bound by Arlon Printers Limited
ISBN 0 946273 22 7

NODDIES

(The Film Extra's Guide)

by

MIKE MARTIN

ABOUT THE AUTHOR

From an early age, Mike Martin wanted to be a feature film director. The son of an established comedian and scriptwriter, he spent three years at art college studying film and television production. Original ambitions thwarted, he drifted more into the performing side of show-business in various bands and acts and as a solo performer, until, by chance, he stumbled upon the work to be found as a background artiste or extra.

He is married, has two sons and lives in Essex.

Mike Martin

THIS BOOK IS DEDICATED TO MY 'EXTRA'
FRIENDS AND ALL THOSE OTHER
BLURRED SHAPES WHOSE CONTRIBUTION
TO THE FILM AND TELEVISION
INDUSTRY HAS BEEN SO FORGETTABLE.

CONTENTS

FOREWORD

In 1951, as a young actor and singer, I managed to get into a show called "The Glorious Days". It was a vehicle for Anna Neagle – who at that time was a huge star – and put on by her husband Herbert Wilcox. No expense was spared. It had a cast of 75 actors and singers, a huge orchestra, and enough scenery to fill a fleet of pantechnicons.

Jimmy Perry OBE

The story-line of the show covered thirty years, and Anna played Nell Gwynne, Queen Victoria (young and old), and a famous musical comedy actress called Kate Something-or-other. She sang a whole host of numbers, and in one – to quote the late and great theatre critic James Agate – 'indulged in a little skirt dancing'.

This was going to be my big break. I never stopped changing costume and wigs for the host of different characters I played:

"cheeky cockney sailor"	6 lines
"cheeky cockney taxi driver"	3 lines
"young soldier in the trenches" 1916	8 lines
"theatrical impressario" (well padded)	7 lines
"an old waiter"	12 lines, no less
"a low-life ruffian"	2 lines

But to cap it all, in the scene of The Restoration, just before King Charles made a big entrance with Nell Gwynne on his arm, I pushed my way to the front of the packed stage, dressed as a Cavalier, with breeches, hose, ribbons and feathers – in fact the full monte – and brandishing a pewter tankard (empty), sang solo these immortal words:

"Drink up, my gay Cavaliers,
Charlie is back on the throne.
Gone are the desolate years.
The King has come into his o-o-o-own"

i

The show toured for nine months, and subsequently came into the Palace Theatre in London.

One of the highlights of "The Glorious Days" was an Investiture scene in which a very old Queen Victoria awarded the VC to a drummer boy for a brave deed in the Zulu wars. Pretty well every member of the cast were on stage in magnificent uniform, including 'yours truly'.

It had been decided that we needed an extra ten officers to fill the scene out, and Herbert Wilcox suggested we pick up "Supers", as he called them, – (the theatrical term for extras that had been used since the days of Sir Henry Irving), in each town we visited. 'And I don't want any nancy boys. Get big firemen and coppers', said Herbert Wilcox.

Anna had a wonderful rapport with audiences and the opening night in Glasgow was received with tremendous enthusiasm. As the lights came up on the Investiture scene, I looked across the stage at the new 'Supers' – all splendid Glasgow firemen, – real men. I noticed one in particular stood out from the others. He was tall, dark, well-built, with a single black eyebrow right across his forehead. 'I suppose he thinks this is a short cut to becoming an actor' I thought patronisingly. 'How pathetic!' However, within a year the Glasgow fireman with one eyebrow became Sean Connery.

So turn the pages of this entertaining book, and let Mike Martin take you into the twilight world of fantasy, humiliation, madness, and all the glamour of Show Business.

Jimmy Perry

ENTERING THE WORLD OF NOD

As a youth I would sit in front of a television or cinema screen wondering just who the hell these people could be. The Arab horde attacking Fort Zinderneuf, the enemy ranks dying so obligingly and in huge numbers by the hero's gun, the crowd in the pub, or simply the poor faceless naff passing by while the principals delivered the dramatic goods.

It seemed an odd occupation. Were they actually paid to do it, I wondered?

My first experience of the whole bizarre business of extra work came when I was a teenage art student. I harboured high ambitions in those days. Attending film school I wanted to be a director. Instead, having volunteered to help out on a local film project, I found myself barefoot in some brambles dressed as a muddied seventeenth century oaf.

I had started the day in full Cromwellian armour, complete with a brace of pistols, carbine, sword and a pair of boots which could have accommodated my entire family. Unable to move, let alone mount a horse (nobody had thought to ask me if I could ride), I was demoted to the rank of peasant. Stripped of all save a pair of ragged breeches, a hair shirt and a hat which must have given rise to the expression 'Dickhead', I was left to fend for myself. The unit all vanished into the distance in various vehicles and I spent the next hour hopping through the gorse before I found the next location. With a bunch of other unfortunates, I was put straight to work building a Digger's commune. After a Spartan lunch of bread and broth, we spent the afternoon getting massacred by yelling Roundhead cavalrymen.

My reward? A begrudged lift to the station. I decided that the real Diggers must have had it easy.

Of course, this was an untypical situation. The film was Kevin Brownlow's COMRADE JACOB, a British Film Institute production on a limited budget and they had scrounged free labour from any source they could. When I entered the realm of big league movies I was soon to find that things could get much worse.

My own circumstances were a bit unsettled. I emerged from college with a diploma in film and television production, but unable to obtain a coveted A.C.T.T. union ticket which would allow me to work in the industry, I partook of a variety of past-times. Initially, I signed on at the benefit office as a film director but the authorities swiftly altered this to 'casual labourer'.

Ego deflated, I tried a few jobs ranging from warehouseman, lorry loader, washer upper and shop assistant, none of which exactly helped to advance my Hitchcockian ambitions. I worked in the entertainment departments of various holiday centres hi-de-hi-ing like crazy. (And there lies a book in its own right!) With my brother Ray, I attempted to form a partnership with a seedy showbiz agent but should have smelt a rat when he offered me a lift and the door of his car came off in my hand. We had to book a hall to audition girls for dancing work abroad but this ended up as a meaty scandal splashed over the front page of the local rag. The church warden who had rented us the room went all bug eyed and spluttery. He must have read our advertisement asking for 'Exotic Dancers' as 'Erotic'. I'm not sure if he was outraged or disappointed. Anyway, all the fuss put paid to that little venture and Lord Grade could now sleep easy.

Born into a showbusiness family (my father was a variety performer), the holiday camps had awakened a dormant desire in me to tread the boards and, being a ham at heart, I had been involved in all sorts of shows and loopy stunts during those eventful summer seasons. At the end of one season, along with my brother again and a friend, we tried to revive an act which we had performed with some success one evening a week to the chips and lager brigade.

The 'Bar Steward's Trio' lasted for exactly one performance in some dodgy London pub. Dressed in boaters, aprons, false handlebar moustaches and soppy grins, we marched on stage to the strains of 'Goodbye Dolly Gray'. I distinctly recall catching a remark from a member of our audience, a drunken harridan who shrieked 'They must be fucking joking!' This was before we had even reached the microphones! So, it seemed that what had wowed Skegness repulsed the outside world.

In an attempt to establish myself in the big city, I took a job in the advertising department of a trade newspaper. I grew to hate this job

*3rd from left ...
as a Butlin's Redcoat.*

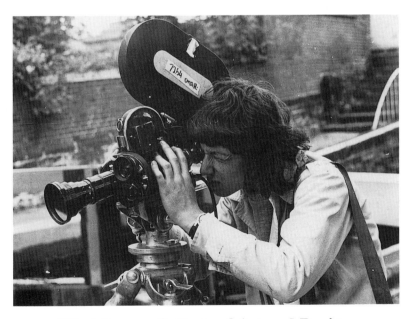

West Surrey College of Art and Design
As a serious student of the art of film making,
how was I to know what lay ahead of me?

We took ourselves so seriously .....

**Directing my diploma television production.
Seems I've been working my way down ever since!**

with a passion, resenting my boss who was always telling me that I had a 'future' with the company. This was the last thing I wanted. The image I had of myself as the next Kubrick was slipping further from my grasp.

I started playing semi-pro in a band and this led on to regular work in a duo, but most of it was a soul destroying round of pubs and clubs. Yet still I refused to succumb to domesticity. And then, the break I needed, or so I thought. A work mate sowed the seeds of my next project. I had an Equity card so why not use it to do film and television background work?

Well, this had occured to me once since my woeful experience on COMRADE JACOB. During the publicity that surrounded the making of Richard Attenborough's war epic, A BRIDGE TOO FAR, I had written to the film company in the hope of getting a few weeks work in Holland as a paratrooper or something. Ignorant of the fact that this was not how such things were done, I was somewhat peeved to be turned down. However, I now had a contact who would show me the initial ropes. The rest is history.

I embarked on a weird road which to date has lasted nearly twenty years. Being a professional extra is like a drug. It has its ups and downs but most of all it instils in those who do it regularly a unique attitude, like a breed apart. I am convinced that there is no other profession on earth to compare with it.

I had a row at the office, resigned and took a temporary job as a stop gap while I prepared for my plunge into the world of extras. Strangely enough, this job was for a major film company, Twentieth Century Fox actually, but there was nothing prestigious about it. I was based in the post room and acted as general go-fer to a bunch of so called 'important' film executives. One day I was sent to buy some special cigars as a present for some visiting moghul. Usually I paid for these things myself then claimed it back from petty cash. After all, I had a tenner on me.

The very sophisticated Soho tobacconists made a great show of presenting this score of cigars in a beautiful gift box, then promptly charged me £98 for them! (Bear in mind this was 1979. You would probably need to take out a mortgage to get them now.) Rattling the change in my pocket, I mumbled some excuse about leaving my wallet in my car, then made my embarrassed way back to the Mr. Big who had ordered them. When I told him the price he drawled, 'Is that all'?

Anyway, I suffered five weeks of carrying out demeaning errands (once I even had to go and buy a pair of replacement underpants for a maintenance man who had messed himself!) while I knocked together an inflated C.V., had photographs taken and contacted all the relevant agents. Then I clinched my first engagement, direct from the B.B.C., as a stand-in on TOP OF THE POPS. Well, this was more like it.

Six of us were employed to stand in during camera rehearsals for any artistes who had failed to arrive. This usually involved gyrating madly to ape the movements of the absent members of the various bands, etc., not always easy if you had to be a convincing Sheena Easton or the like. We also had to learn the camera movements so that during the evening recording we could prevent the kids in the studio audience from being decapitated by the scything cranes.

My fellow stand-ins that first day were a mixed crew. A fringe theatre director who spent most of the many spare moments writing a play, a bitter comic whose cynicism knew no bounds, a surly bruiser of unknown origin and some identical twin brothers who were later to find fame, of a sort, in a situation comedy series. (Remember the twin yellow coats in HI-DE-HI?)

My second job was on Trevor Eve's private eye series SHOESTRING. I had to pour wine for a group of actors in a party scene but succeeded in pouring most of it down Michael Medwin's sleeve. Then I went off on location (Notting Hill!) for some play, and my role involved walking past a window with my coat collar turned up. I was released after forty minutes and got paid more for that than it would have taken me to earn in two days at the newspaper. This was money for old rope. I was hooked.

I decided that there must be a lucrative living to be made here. Never having really thought about it before, I realised that there were endless programmes, films and commercials always in production and they would forever be in need of bodies to fill in the background action. Also, green as I was, I reasoned that there must be a good chance of getting oneself spotted. After all, I would be involved in the day to day

EW1 **BBC tv**

BRITISH BROADCASTING CORPORATION
TELEVISION CENTRE WOOD LANE LONDON W12 7RJ
Tel.: 01-743 8000 : Telex : 265781 Telegrams and Cables : Telecasts London Telex

MIKE VINDEN
BBC Ref. 35/CC

Date   9 MAY 79

Keep

TELEVISION   E 1 EX

1. Artist (Retain)
2. Acceptance (Sign and return)
3. Enterprises P C   4. Prog. Dept.   5. Index   1

This engagement is offered on the terms and conditions set out herein.   Attendances are required as set out below or at any other places or times
the BBC may direct.

EXTRA(S)

PROGRAMME TITLE: TOP OF THE POPS 79

RECORDING DATE(S)(OR LIVE TX) :   9 MAY 79:

PROJECT NO(S): 012491836
DIRECTOR OR PRODUCER: ROBIN NASH

CONTRIBUTION:TO ACT AS STAND-IN AS	STAND-IN FEE	23.00
REQUIRED AT REHEARSALS AND IN		
BRIEF APPEARANCES ALSO TO LEARN	OVERTIME PAYMENT(S) 3 X £2-75P	
CAMERA MOVES		8.25
ACT AS CROWD MARSHALL		
AND TO WORK AS REQ BY P.A:	TOTAL	£31.25

ATTENDANCES REQUIRED:
  10.55AM ONWARDS TVC:

QUERIES RE CHEQUES TO ARTISTS PAYMENTS TELEVISION ACCOUNTS TEL:(01)580 4468

IF REGISTERED, RETURN VAT INVOICE WITH CONTRACT FOR VAT INCLUSIVE PAYMENT.

Signed on behalf of the BBC

E.K. WILSON
HEAD OF ARTISTS' CONTRACTS, TELEVISION)

Authorised for Payment

MIKE VINDEN
C-O MIKE MARTIN
█████████
WALTHAMSTOW
LONDON E17

Normal Country of Residence (if not UK) of each Artist covered hereby.

I ACCEPT this engagement(s) and undertake to observe the terms and conditions set out herein.

Date.................................Artist's Signature....................................
Signed Acceptance to be returned to BBC Signatory at address above.

SOCIAL SECURITY ACTS
State your NATIONAL INSURANCE NUMBER here :-

FAILURE TO DO SO may lead to delay in payment hereunder.

Where applicable, contributions will be deducted at the standard rate
UNLESS a certificate of non or reduced liability is obtained from the
Department of Health and Social Security and supplied to the BBC.

1   PUNCH 0124918 36 VINDA 6 5675 45090 579 C

One of my first television contracts.
The director, Robin Nash, became a top executive at the B.B.C.

7

making of television, wouldn't I? Surely I must meet all the right people, ingratiate myself, touch a forelock...

Poor fool. I was yet to understand the dreaded stigma that is irrevocably attached to extra work. But this realisation lay in the future. Right now I was away. Most of the agents took me on and there seemed to be work in abundance. Over the first few weeks I was a Saxon in King Arthur's Court, a double for Noel Edmonds, A Victorian sailor, a German pop fan, a chorister, a detective, a second for a cooker in a boxing match (work that one out!) and a dancing biscuit, to mention but a few.

Could anyone ask for a more diverse career?

Appearing in
Old Time Music Hall

Can you spot me?

9

CENTRAL CASTING

I joined another union, the Film Artistes Association, whereby I registered with Central Casting and commenced working in films too.

Unlike television, film work did not require Equity membership. In T.V., you always knew (at that time) that the people you were working with were (or had been) involved in showbusiness somewhere along the line, be they failed actors, variety artistes filling in, or retired acrobatic barrel jumpers, but films made no such distinctions. The F.A.A. took people on depending upon age and type, whatever they needed at the time. Consequently, on film sets you would find yourself mixing with characters from all walks of life; taxi drivers and market traders (lots of these supplementing their incomes), housewives, all kinds of ordinary folk, plus yobs, weirdos, layabouts, conmen and, I kid you not, even ex gangsters. A lot of heavy, dubious types appeared to be attracted to the easy money and some of them even ended up working as minders for visiting star names. They had their own code too, which seemed to translate as 'Get in my way at your peril'. I soon realised that certain assistant directors (that is, the people with the job of liaison between extras and the powers that be) appeared to be intimidated by them. You could see it in the completely inappropriate casting of some productions.

For instance, on one film two hundred disco dancers were needed. This was the age of new wave/punk rock and the company were paying an extra ten pounds to all those who came dressed for the part. The place was filled with Mohican haircuts, garrish make-up, condom ear-rings and bondage trousers, but not being of punkish persuasion I merely made a limited effort. However, at least I was of the right age group, unlike a score of the crowd who were middle aged, pot bellied, tattooed, flat nosed and battle scarred. This bunch could ride themselves in on any call. I swear, if Zefferelli wanted cygnets for SWAN LAKE they would be there.

At the end of the day we queued for our money. (Unlike television, film work almost always used to pay cash on the spot.) A cube like wedge of nastiness elbowed his way into the line ahead of me and I didn't feel inclined to protest. In front of him was a leather clad youth whose appearance resembled a Nazi peacock. Quite rightly this youth received his tenner. When it came to our Prince Charming, the assistant authorised his pay chit for basic money.

'Wot der fuck's this?' bellowed Parkhurst's answer to the Poet Laureate.

'Your chit,' quaked the assistant nervously.

'Wot about that arse'ole?' roared the charmer, throwing a ham like fist in the direction of the punk, 'Why'd e' get money on top?'

'He was dressed colourfully.'

'So? I've got a fuckin' red shirt on, en' I?'

True, he did. You could almost see the scarlet beneath the brick dust. I suppose he wore it so that the blood wouldn't show. He got his money.

On that same film, I first witnessed the stark contrast between extra and star. Burt Reynolds, in his luxury trailer, sipping aperitifs while the rest of us queued for a mobile lunch in the rain.

Hazel O'Connor's BREAKING GLASS involved over a thousand people at an outdoor rock concert. Owing to the numbers needed, many of the crowd were not even F.A.A. members and had been employed direct from squats. ('Do you want to be in a film?'.... that kind of thing.) Skinheads and reprobates most of them, to play a National Front mob. The rest of us were supposed to be enjoying a 'Rock Against Racism' concert when we come under attack. Fake bricks and other assorted dummy weapons had been issued, but it wasn't long before the real thing started to zip through the air. In the first take I found myself in the front line with a baying mob bearing down on me. Suddenly I realised how the British infantrymen must have felt when they faced the Zulus at Isandwlhana!

It was a very hairy and bruising experience. Those skinheads really meant business and were taking full advantage of their legalised dust up. By take two I was hiding behind a wall (amongst other fugitives) where I spent the rest of the day.

Another incident worth mentioning took place on a commercial. As a rule, Casting did not book commercials but this was an exception. It

1st. Assistant

3rd. Assistant

2nd. Assistant

Mike Martin.

was for a well known tabloid newspaper promoting their new bingo game. About a hundred of us were crammed into the set gathered around Jimmy Tarbuck. After he had breathlessly extolled the virtues of the game, the heavens opened and we were to be showered with money, leaping around and waving our arms in ecstasy.

Now, for some inexplicable reason, they decided to use real money. There must have been a few grand in assorted notes, fresh from the bank, crisp in their packets. Two prop men were assigned to sprinkle this rich rain upon us from the studio gantry and straight away the wiser among us could see trouble ahead.

I tried to keep out of the way as the cash came fluttering down for take after take, getting grubbier each time as the prop men scooped it up in armfuls to send it down again and again. It was going everywhere. Incredibly, at the end of the day only about ninety pounds was missing which I thought to be a miracle. I took it for granted that the authorities would be lucky to retrieve a fiver. Anyway, we were given a terrible drubbing, accused of theft and threatened with having our fees docked to make up the loss! Naturally, we countered with the suggestion that if any accusations were to be levelled, why should the finger not also be pointed at the prop men? Didn't they have an ideal scapegoat? But, of course, the general feeling was that if there were any thieves about they had to be amongst the extras. I'm pleased to say that the company eventually decided to swallow their losses and pay the price for their own stupidity. After all, on screen nobody would have been able to tell the difference if bits of cut up wallpaper were floating down.

I also recall a time when hundreds of us, dressed as World War Two British soldiers, swamped Nine Elms railway yard in Battersea (the film was EYE OF THE NEEDLE) as Donald Sutherland made his entrance hanging on the front of a steam engine. During the shooting breaks scores of 'soldiers' in various stages of undress and slovenliness could be seen spilling out onto the street, ambling to the telephone box or the pub. An off duty military policeman who happened to be passing was outraged and tried to get the production stopped on the grounds that we were debasing the image of the British Army. He even went so far as contacting his commanding officer but by the time he had generated any support we had wrapped for the day.

Once, Casting sent me to the Tower of London for a day on something called THE SCREAMERS. Must be a horror film, thought I, but no... it was a German soap opera! The von Screamer family... ja!

EXTRA TYPES

AGENTS

If you mean business and intend to make a living out of this unreliable profession, you must be registered with several agents and always have your nose to the ground. There are agents dealing almost exclusively with background work, in fact too many nowadays as it has spread the available work too thinly.

In days gone by, one would just have a quick meeting with a new agent and supply some photographs, but now the agents all produce their own casting books, entry into which can cost anything from about £60 to over £100. If you are with several of them, as so many of us have to be, these books set you back a small fortune as most are reprinted annually. And it still doesn't stop them sending you into town for auditions just to have a polaroid taken. One asks, what are these books for? (Silly question. Obviously someone is making a lot of money out of them. High printing costs? Pah!!!)

Once you are with an agent there is no absolute guarantee of work. I know of people who have paid their money and never had a single job. However, as long as you have all your limbs and at least one brain cell you should be employed at least occasionally. You see, most of the work does not require a high level of intellect. If you are adept at merging into the background, can mumble 'Rhubarb' and have a presentable left ear or shoulder, you should go far.

All agents have their own system, I suppose, but there seems to be no pattern in the distribution of jobs. Sometimes you will not hear from some of them for weeks or even months, then suddenly they will ring and offer you several days on different things. (Usually just as you have decided not to cough up for another year in their book, thus creating a dilemma.)

And, of course, you must check in. Checking in is like a religion to the serious noddy. (Noddy being the affectionate euphemism for extra.) This requires telephoning the agents several times a week to remind them that you are still alive. You must get used to the familiar refrains of 'nothing suitable' or 'ring tomorrow' but that is the name of the game. Sometimes you can strike lucky, catch them at just the right moment and find yourself employed.

Speaking personally, one or two agents have been my mainstay over the years, and I have been fortunate enough to work fairly regularly for them, even pulling in an occasional 'feature'. To be featured in a commercial is a noddy's dream as this means residual payments. In the world of advertising this can be very handsome indeed.

It is rare, though not unknown, to be booked on a commercial as a background artiste on a daily rate, then to be lucky enough to find yourself placed in shot in just the right position to warrant a feature. (i.e. Recognisable in directed action, relevant to the plot, handling the product, etc.. The Equity agreement says something along these lines.)

If the commercial is then networked nationally, and maybe abroad too, your money accumulates through a complicated system of regions, categories and showings and you can end up with oodles of cash. As I say, this is rare. I have had quite a few near misses, some of which I thought were obvious ones, while others, which I never dreamed would pay off, did. You see, sometimes the production company will fight tooth and nail to wriggle out of it while on other occasions it seems they can't wait to throw their money at you. Not too long ago I went through the agony of clinching an agreement only to see the company who had employed me go bust! The irony was that loads of people thought I had already earned a King's ransom from it. It's a funny old business. Usually the director will do his utmost to keep you out of shot, aware as he is of the pound signs in your eyes. Sometimes you might have auditioned and been booked as a featured artiste anyway (although such bona fide work belongs to the more reputable theatrical agencies as a rule) but usually it is just pot luck. Yes, one of those nebulous things that keeps so many of us in the game when deep down we know we should be doing something more worthwhile with our lives.

When I think of some of the things I have done to further the cause of advertising it makes me wince. I have been shot at and hacked by pirates, run over by chariots, immersed in icy water, marooned on scaffolding, led blindfold through a marsh whilst singing 'Hi ho, hi ho!', been forced to chomp endless chocolate bars whilst on the run and been dressed in animal skins and antlers to charge headlong into a barn in an attempt to batter it down! (This last one was to promote cream crackers. What else?) Think about it too deeply and it's like

THE OLD PRO "2"

being on some mind expanding substance.

Still, there are worse ways to make a living. I must add that certain jobs have been sheer Heaven. Excellent food, nice treatment, beautiful locations (say, at a stately home on a fine summer's day, for example). So there is a positive side to it all. (What's this? Not complaining? Can't have worked for a while...)

Getting back to the point, I must stress again that the serious noddy really must get into the habit of pestering the agents as one is easily forgotten and totally replaceable.

Hitting a quiet patch is deadly. When one goes a few days without work, a professional extra begins to take it personally. He/she will start to feel that they have been abandoned. 'What's wrong with me?' they whine. They take to scouring every inch of their television screens searching for familiar de-focussed faces, then on finding one howl 'Bastard! Why didn't **I** get that job?' The only remedy is to phone round your compatriots until you find someone who is doing even worse. Great tonic that.

There is a lady who works in one of the agent's offices who has become something of a legend. At one time she manned the phone at Central Casting which I guess must have had an effect on her. Personally, I like the woman. She's straight and doesn't waffle, but a lot of people are phased by her dead pan, monotone, nasal delivery. She wastes no time in getting to the point. Once she rang and asked me if I had a dinner jacket. When I told her I had she hung up. Presumably, if I hadn't had one I would have got the job.

A production about a legendary outlaw was shooting in the West Country and she asked one startled chap if he had been 'down on Robin Hood'. 'No,' he replied, 'it's a filthy rumour.'

Somebody else was asked, 'Have you been on A NICE GIRL LIKE ME?'

She has a classic line. Many have laid claim to being the one to whom she uttered this gem, so I wonder if it is actually true. If not it should be because it sums her up to a tee. Quote; 'Have you still got blue eyes?'

Another agent would always say 'I won't forget you, cocker' when he couldn't even remember your name. And another, now deceased, was always full of charm, a real gentleman who would promise to put you on the very next thing that came in as if you were the only one on his books. Then you wouldn't hear from him for months.

One girl, having been with a particular agency for several months without receiving a single call was finally contacted and asked if she could get to a West End hotel within the hour. She said she could but was then told that she wouldn't be needed for long as her job merely entailed setting out the chairs for a conference! Not quite what she had in mind for her acting career.

Someone else was offered two days from another agent for whom he had never worked. The fee? Nothing. It was for the 'Save the Seals' campaign.

On odd occasions moral blackmail is used in this way to get extras to do charity work. Now don't get me wrong. Charity is commendable and fine to do as an artiste because then the gesture means something. Asking extras to do it is another matter because I don't feel that it is appreciated. The attitude seems to be 'Silly sods. They'll do anything for a free meal'.

Another ploy is to be offered work at a reduced fee, usually excused by 'They're a new company... not much money... do this and they'll remember you'. Yes indeed. Remember you as a twat. Never underprice yourself, regardless of the temptation to earn a shekel. The argument 'You might as well do it if you're not doing anything else' is a sham. Work for a shilling today and it will be sixpence tomorrow as did, in fact, happen. More of that later.

In more recent times, a number of ex-extras have thrown in the towel and presumably thinking 'If you can't beat 'em, join 'em', have started their own agencies. One or two have done okay, but for the most part I would rather be represented by a termite.

There are literally dozens of agencies now. When I started, a mere handful dealt with all the available work and it paid to be registered with them all. These days choosing an agent must be a chaotic nightmare. They seem to pick odd names for themselves too, sometimes bordering on the surreal. 'The Ugly Agency', 'Joe Public', 'Ordinary

People', 'Bovver Boots' and 'Snowshaft'. What the hell is 'Snowshaft'? Or grandiose names like 'Action Personnel'. This last agent has had several changes of name. Now it is split into two sections called, less flamboyantly, G1 and G2. You can only be registered with one or the other, apparently, as 1 is for prestigious, featured type of work and 2 is for extras. Never the twain shall meet.

One agency was even run by an ex R.A.F. flight sergeant. He was a bombastic, military type who once said to me, 'Do you know why I'm so successful in this business? Because I was never in the bloody business, that's why! I'm a business**man**!'

When I was going for my initial interview with him, everybody told me that he wouldn't approve of the long hair and beard I was sporting at the time. So, prepared for this, I straightaway said to him, 'I realise the hair and beard limits me for work...'

He countered without hesitation, saying, 'On the contrary. You're a character! I'll have you working seven days a week!'

He thumbed through my pictures then tossed them contemptuously onto his desk.

'Mind you,' he grunted, 'these photographs will have to be changed. That one of you with the guitar... you look like some bloody rocker!'

So, at considerable expense, I had another batch of Denbry repros printed with the offending picture removed. When I took them back to him the first thing he said was, 'That bloody beard and hair will hold you back. Clean shaven with a nice short back and sides I could have you working seven days a week!'

Another one of the main agencies was run by an outrageous Welsh queen who used to work as a photographic model. He used to thrive on using innuendo whenever he rang with a job. I was never sure if he was serious but it was always very tiresome.

'Oh, hello Mike. Did I get you out of bed? Are you free on the night of the twelfth? Don't worry, it's work not a proposition...'

Other blokes were asked to measure their members along the length of the telephone. How very professional. Before I met him, several

"You look like some bloody Rocker!"
MIKE VINDEN is my Equity persona, Vinden being my
Romany Grandmother's maiden name.

**WAITING FOR THE
REMAKE OF "GREASE"**
(Photograph by Martin Haskell)

21

people had told me that he had given them a hard time at their interviews; making lewd suggestions, asking them to sit next to him, touching them up and so on. With this in mind, I hauled on a pair of chain mail Y fronts and set off to see him.

Actually, the interview was very straight, seated in his office with his irritating little dogs yelping at my heels. He worked from home, a tastefully decorated flat, full of antiques. As I was leaving and thinking 'Thank God, he doesn't fancy me', he suddenly called out, 'Hold it a moment. Slip your jacket off.'

Very warily, I took one arm out of my sleeve as he creepily approached me. Without a word he started poking and grabbing at my waist. Tensing up I demanded to know what he was doing.

He drew away immediately. 'Oh, I just thought you were a little podgy, that's all.'

An old duo partner of mine (we once had an act together called 'Mus n' Grumble' and I make no apologies for that!) thought it would be a good idea to take his little boy to see this agent with the intention of getting the whole family working. Unfortunately, the young mite, only being about two years of age, did not show a lot of decorum and ran about like a whirlwind amidst the Welsh queen's valuables. 'Mind that vase! Oh no, the sideboard! Look, I really don't think you should let him run around like that.'

Not wishing to offend, Grumble (or was it Mus?) swooped down to grab the lad. Swinging him up into his arms, he leaned back and promptly smashed the back of his head through the glass face of an antique clock!

Whilst on the subject of children, I will say a few words about their working potential. On odd occasions children are needed for film shoots but they do tend to get paid only about half money as a rule. My own two boys have appeared in a few things but I wouldn't like them to get too involved in the background business. One of them loved playing the devil's henchman in T.V. HELL with Angus Deayton and Paul Merton. When they were both much smaller we were booked as a family for a crowd scene on a cigar commercial. I was a bit concerned about how to keep their enthusiasm up for two days on a hot, boring set but I needn't have worried. Blackpool beach had been recreated on a Shepperton sound stage, complete with sand, donkey rides, entertainment and endless free supplies of junk food. They had a whale of a time.

There are actually laws restricting the amount of hours children are permitted to work but these rules are often ignored and the kids exploited. It's up to the parents or chaperones to put a foot down about it because when the time is up, they are perfectly within their rights to leave the set regardless of the production schedules. I have seen children worked through the night in horrible conditions but the greed of their guardians is to blame for that.

I was with my boys once on a big shoot at a sports stadium. The boys seemed happy enough playing with the other kids and exploring but after a few hours I decided that I had had enough and was going to exercise my rights. Seeking out the assistant I told him, 'Look, you've had the kids for way past their time. I'm afraid I'm going to have to take them home.'

'You can't do that. We need them for the next shot.'

'Sorry. You've had them long enough. They're bored, tired and hungry and we're leaving now.'

The boys, who were at my side, heard this and began to wail, 'No, dad, we like it here!' much to the amusement of the assistant. It's great to have allies.

Another job with the boys involved two days of thrills and spills at Chessington World of Adventures for a Beecham's Powders commercial. They enjoyed themselves immensely but the most attractive thing to me was the money involved which was fairly considerable. Imagine my distress when, a few weeks later, the agent informed me that the film company concerned had gone bust and we were not going to receive a penny!

The boys, having watched me rant and rave about this, sobered my mood with their wide eyed innocence.

'Never mind, dad,' said the elder one, 'at least we got into Chessington for free!'

The younger one has always shown signs of being a real ham and I think it very likely that he will end up pursuing some kind of showbiz career. I just hope that he has seen enough of the lower end of the business to keep him out of the noddy ranks when he gets older.

EXTRA TYPES

The Failed Model

AUDITIONS

You may be astonished to know that auditions are not normally needed for the casting of extras. Having said that, there are times when one is sent on a special trip into town, forced to wait an age in some thick piled reception, to be received by some arty type who stares, prods and usually views one as an object rather than as a human being. Then you may be ordered to stand in front of a video camera, front view and profile like a convict, and utter your name and purpose. More often than not, however, you will be in and out in thirty seconds, just time enough to have a polaroid snap taken. From this you may be engaged to appear as a left shoulder in a beer commercial.

I have had some odd auditions. There was one which was for a shoot in Barcelona. Three impassive Spaniards, all unable to speak a word of English, sat glaring at me as I perched upon a stool, told by the production assistant that they were looking for a comical newscaster.

'Be funny,' she instructed me.

Then there was the time I was asked if I did any judo or karate. Some years prior to this I had turned up to enrol for a martial arts course but had changed my mind, leaving before I got my shoes off.

'Judo and karate? Of course,' I brashly replied.

You see, I was, by now, wise enough to know that you don't talk yourself out of a job too quickly. Several times before I had turned down work by being honest. 'Can you play tennis? Shove ha'penny? The glockenspiel?' Then you find out that some moron bluffed it for the sake of the special skills payment and no one was any the wiser. As long as you can draw breath it seems to be enough to qualify you for 90% of the work. So, off I went to the audition.

It was an ordinary office. Just the director and a muscular individual in judo rig, complete with black belt.

'Been fighting long?' he asked.

'Er... not that long...' I mumbled, rapidly realising that I might have dropped an almighty one.

He frowned and handed me a judo jacket and belt and told me to put them on. Now, how was I supposed to know that there is a special way of donning these things? I think he sussed me as soon as I delicately tied it around myself in a kind of granny knot. He was irritated now because I was wasting his time. Walking behind me, he asked if I could throw him over my shoulder. Next thing I knew I was skidding across the floor on my backside and slamming into the wall.

'Try it faster,' he grinned sadistically.

Having flung me around the office for a while, he let me limp away. And I didn't get the job. Funny that.

Not being a dancer, I was amazed that I passed an audition to dance the minuet in a commercial. As a musician I think my sense of rhythm is fine, but for some reason I have always had a problem with co-ordination between my brain and feet. Unfortunately, this commercial required perfect synchronisation between several couples in a ballroom sequence and I'm afraid I made a complete pig's ear out of it. During rehearsals, the choreographer grew so exasperated with my efforts that she hit me with her script. If they wanted Wayne Sleep they should have booked him!

One of my favourite memories, now that it's long gone, must be of the time when I impersonated a walrus. An agent asked if I minded working in a skin. Well, I had done this kind of thing before. (BLAKE'S SEVEN immediately sprang to mind when I had played a hairy mutant, and caught a make-up generated skin disease into the bargain.) This one would be very lucrative if I got it, for it was to be a featured part in a commercial, even though I would be encased in fur.

There were dozens at the audition; dancers and midgets galore. My turn came and I walked into a lush office. A group of people faced me over a huge desk, the director, his P.A., the producer, a couple of advertising reps and clients...

'Now then,' said the director, 'we've two parts left to cast. The theme is ALICE IN WONDERLAND. There's the hare; young, vibrant... or the walrus, old, plodding, seen better days... which do you see yourself as?'

I'd had a late night so I opted for the walrus.

'Right. Well, he does do a dance...'

So, without the aid of costume or music I gave them my interpretation of a walrus dancing. It was the longest twenty seconds of my life. My audience was completely humourless as they watched me shuffling around like a demented drunk with his heels nailed to the floor. Every now and then they would mutter to one another or scribble some notes. I slowed down.

'Carry on... carry on...' they urged.

And so I did, expecting Jeremy Beadle to emerge from a cupboard at any moment. At last they let me finish. Red faced I eyed the door but they weren't going to let me escape that easily.

'He also plays snooker,' I was informed by the straight faced client.

Deciding that the whole thing must be a wind up, I humoured them and let my last trace of dignity evaporate. Then they took a polaroid! I thought they might ask me to grow two teeth to tusk length.

As I closed the door on them I was surprised not to hear group laughter echoing down the corridor. I went home thinking that I had completely wasted my time.

Amazingly, I got it. Must be a lesson there somewhere.

**MY
INFAMOUS
WALRUS
IMPRESSION**

**GULLIVER
IN
LILLIPUT
(B.B.C.)**

PAY

The money for background work is paid via a complicated system of various rates. Basically, and it always seems to be changing, the television companies have agreements with Equity. Until quite recently these agreements were enforcable by law but nowadays they only serve as a guide. Independent smaller companies can now offer what they like, but I will get to that in more detail later. As for the larger concerns (i.e. the big commercial channels like Thames, etc.) they still have guidelines but they differ from the B.B.C.. For instance, job titles have altered.

A lot of extras began to object to being called what they were. True, there is something demeaning about the word 'extra', especially when some assistants cough it out whilst practically holding their noses in disgust. So, 'extra' became 'supporting artiste'. This was the lowest position, but the next grade up was 'Walk On 1'. Here lay a grey area. 'Walk On 1' was supposed to be granted if the 'supporting artiste' had been singled out for personal direction, i.e. a reaction or serving drinks, etc.. Financially, the difference to the daily rate was only a few pounds, but the real reward came if the programme was repeated, for then the 'Walk On 1' was entitled to 100% repayment of his/her original fee.

Next step for the lucky ones was a 'Walk On 2', which was given if the 'Walk On 1' was asked to utter a few words of unscripted dialogue. ('You rang, sir?', 'The enemy is without...' etc., etc..) Anything more than that and you would be in the realms of drama contracts. Then the world is your oyster; oversea's sales, respect, the lot!

Just to complicate matters, the independent television companies do not have 'supporting artistes'. They start with 'Walk On 1' but at the same money (give or take a pound or two) as the B.B.C.'s 'supporting artiste', and without repeats. To get the equivalent of the BEEB's 'Walk On 1', you have to get an I.T.V. 'Walk On 2' and for a 'Walk On 2' you need a 'Walk On 3'! Are you still with me? (At least, that's the way it was...)

Film work was completely different. Once again, the situation has changed immensely, but for years films were not answerable to Equity.

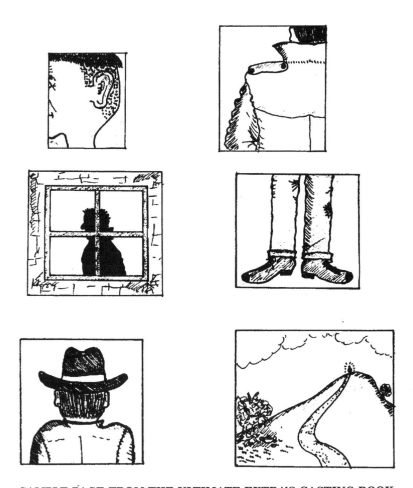

SAMPLE PAGE FROM THE ULTIMATE EXTRA'S CASTING BOOK

M.M.

Instead there was the F.A.A. agreement. (You had to be a member.) In the past this arrangement was an open book for anyone with a bit of front and negotiating skills but producers gradually got wise and the rules were changed. You see, film money was almost always paid in cash at the end of the day. Not only that, but anything extra you might have done was negotiable on top of the basic pay. So, a typical scenario with a 'Jack the Lad' versus an assistant might go like this:

Extra: 'I fink there's some special (special action) to go on that, guvn'r.'

Assistant (tiredly): 'Why, what did you do?'

Extra: 'Well, there was just me an' Robert Mitchum in that shot after lunch. I 'ad to 'and 'im 'is fags. The director told me to do it.'

Assistant: 'Oh yes, I remember. You weren't really seen, were you... I'll give you a fiver on top.'

Extra: 'Do me a favour! I 'ad a line an' reaction, an' all. Call it thirty.'

Assistant: 'Get out of here! I'll give you ten.'

Extra: 'Twenty.'

Assistant (with a sigh of resignation): 'Alright. Done.'

Extra (chuckling to himself): 'You 'ave bin, my son. Now... wot abaht wet money? (Working in the rain) An' the body make-up, an' broken supper?'

And so on. It was sometimes possible, if handled right, to make a small fortune on a single day's chit.

Obviously the system was open to abuse. The more belligerent you were, the more you stood to make. Arguments were forever raging over who did what, so a new agreement was drawn up which caused near riots for a while. Additional payments were now to be grouped from A to E, from about £5 to £30, and you could only be awarded one of these categories at a time. Previously, if you were on horseback in the rain, wearing a beard and itchy costume whilst singing the national anthem, you stood to make enough to pay off your mortgage. The new agreement would include one set payment to cover the lot.

**THE
KENNY
EVERETT
SHOW
(B.B.C.)**

**KISSING
THE COX
OF THE
CREW!**

Also, week-end work used to be desirable as the daily rate went up by about a third if you were fortunate enough to be called on a Saturday or Sunday. Now, however, they pay the same as any other day. Another perk that vanished was the system whereby you could get extra overtime by deliberately taking your time in the paying off queue. When I was green, I used to think people were being so polite by allowing me to go in front of them, when really they were just trying to nick another hour's money. This was replaced by a complete free for all the moment the first assistant announced 'Wrap!'. (End of the day's shooting.) Orderly queues became a thing of the past as desperate extras tried all manner of ploys to get dealt with first. 'Jibbing' (queue jumping) became a kind of art form, ranging from the subtle elbow to the downright violent shove.

Nightwork retained its seperate higher rate, and overtime is still pretty generous, along with extra money for early calls, shortened meal breaks and extreme haircuts. So, a film extra could still make a good profit and for quite a while the system remained generally more lucrative than television work, minus the repeat fees.

However, greed can sometimes get the better of you. I always swore I would never overdo things, but I found myself in a position where I had been booked on a night shoot near Pinewood for three nights. At the same time, Casting offered me three days on a T.V. mini series at Shepperton. It would mean working all through the nights, finishing at dawn to make a mad dash to the daytime calls by 7.00am.. Thinking only of the money, I took it.

The first day wasn't too bad, but by the second I was in a bad way. I had been hoping that I would be able to grab odd snippets of shut-eye during the shooting breaks, but, as luck would have it, both productions had particularly tight schedules and I barely had a spare moment. Much of the time floated by in a kind of comatose state. I was half asleep on my feet and how I made the journeys to and fro alive I will never know. (I know a man who actually slumped across the wheel and turned his car over doing something like this.) It took me a good fortnight to recover from this punishment to my metabolism. It simply wasn't worth it.

As I mentioned before, another attractive aspect of film work was the cash on the day, but, once again, such an arrangement was open to the conmen. Arriving on set, extras were given their work chit which they duly filled in and handed back at the end of the day in exchange for their money and green copy. Chits were like gold dust and were guarded closely. Even so, this did not prevent a whole wedge of blank ones from falling into unscrupulous hands. (They were pinched from the back seat of an assistant's car.) The culprit actually managed to queue up for several dollops of cash before he was caught. Actually, he had mis-spelled 'London' on all the fake addresses he had submitted! Where are you Raffles when we need you?

The other main areas of work are in-house videos, training films and photographic modelling. Videos and films for private businesses are subject to minimal rates as a rule, although sometimes it is possible to land a significant part, complete with reams of dialogue, which makes it more interesting. However, to get their money's worth, they will very often work you near to death and your performance will only be seen by the likes of trainee hotel managers in Cleethorpes or salesmen in Penge.

As for photographic work, this is supposed to pay on a very handsome hourly basis. Indeed, sometimes it does, but the agents started offering deals so that the clients could get a whole day's labour at a reduced rate.

I was fortunate to have another avenue of revenue by belonging to the Musician's Union. This meant that when I was employed to appear with a musical instrument, even if it was only miming, I had to be paid a proper musician's session rate. In this way I made a tidy sum on JEEVES AND WOOSTER as a banjo playing, black faced drone. Likewise, a group of us mimed violin playing in a ballroom scene for SCARLETT (the poor man's sequel to GONE WITH THE WIND) and went home with nearly three times as much money as our noddy chums.

My violin playing once got me into a very embarrassing situation. I actually play a very limited country style fiddle, but I can look convincing enough for miming purposes. But there came a time when I was booked, with my fiddle, to perform in a promotional insert for the B.B.C.'s Telethon. I had been told it was merely a visual appearance, but, as is so often the case, that was not to be. We were in a West End London theatre, and there I was, alone on stage, trembling in my white tie and tails as the director asked me to give them about five minutes of classical pieces! I should have come clean, but like a fool, I tried to bluff it. 'Turkey in the Straw' or a bit of Cajun shuffling would have been no problem, but for me to attempt to ape Nigel Kennedy was tantamount to musical suicide. Being nervous didn't help and the stone, stunned silence from the crew and assembled onlookers did nothing to help me through the ordeal. All I could hope for was that they would think I was some kind of eccentric avant garde type of player, but I don't think I managed it. I heard what they did...a kind of scraping, tortured cat sound which bore absolutely no relation to known musical structure. It seemed to go on forever and I shudder to think that the bloody thing is committed to tape somewhere in the B.B.C. vaults. Afterwards, it appeared to me that everyone, who had been so pleasant to me previously, went 'shtum' and couldn't meet my eye. The P.A. mumbled an uncomfortable 'thankyou' and I slunk away, head bowed in shame. Thank God, when it was shown, they didn't use any of the sound track. How could they? In fact, my silent performance accompanied by a 'voice over' was very Menuhin-esque. Just goes to show...

As a rule, most work is followed by a long, long wait for payment. When the job is done, a lengthy process begins when the agent invoices the relevant company, the company mulls it over for a wholly unreasonable period, finally sends the money to the agent who then, having extracted their commission, V.A.T. and handling charge, will at last issue a cheque to the patient artiste who by now may very well have expired of old age or starvation.

This system varies enormously depending upon which agent you have worked for. It is not unknown for certain agents to hang onto your money for some time after they have received it. (Think of the interest on fifty people's wages salted into a building society account for a month.) Some of them only pay out on a set day of the month. If your money arrives from the client the day after this date, then the agent can officially keep your money for another four weeks. By law they are supposed to pay you within ten days of receiving your fee but this just sems to be ignored. Television work usually pays up relatively quickly but commercials can drag on for months. The worst is photographic work as you are dependant upon the conscience of the individual photographer. I know of one reluctant employer who had his equipment seized by some irate heavies who had worked for him. I once waited nearly a year for payment from a Belgian snapper.

A saying has arisen in the noddy game. Work in June and the money will come in handy for Christmas.

THE EXTRA'S BREAKFAST
(Everything in a roll ...)

STIGMA

Unfortunately, a great anti-extra stigma exists in the business. Generally speaking, **proper** actors and actresses, production staff and even the caterers look down on the background artistes, seeing them as idle, complaining, talentless, greedy and a waste of space. A necessary evil. In many cases, I wouldn't deny that this attitude is justifiable.

The problem is that, over the years, a few bad elements have caused everyone to be tarred with the same brush. There are many reasons for this. Unless deeply involved in the aesthetics of a production, no place on earth can end up more tedious than a film or television studio set.

Having arrived at a studio or location, the initial novelty value quickly dulls and once you have visited make-up, wardrobe and had breakfast, the day turns into a seemingly endless mush of hanging about. One can only do so much reading and if you are not fortunate enough to have friends with you, (which can make the day a nice social occasion) it's not that long before the brain starts to go numb, and if you are not careful, you may find yourself falling victim to the dreaded moaning disease. For want of something to talk about, once all the chat about work and agents has been exhausted, groups of extras take to complaining about anything they can think of. Initially, this can be the tedium, the food (although it is usually pretty good), the attitude of the assistants, speculation of finishing time, then gradually it turns into a kind of bizarre nitpicking. 'Oh, I wish I hadn't had that third piece of gateaux... they really shouldn't lay on wine for us... makes me so sleepy in the afternoons... this seat is too soft... I'll be awake all night...' and so on.

Naturally, the crew pick up on this. They see us, most of the time, as ungrateful, lazy, pig-like bleeders who pinch all the food. Of course, many an overweight crew member will be saying these things inbetween belches whilst cramming a whole chicken into his mouth. Many of them suffer from their own affliction, 'Location Belly' or 'Grip's Gut', brought on by long term exposure to mobile catering units. Also, their I.Q. and behaviour can leave a lot to be desired. I had the sophisticated experience, on a public street, of having to witness the loutish enthusiasm of a group of crew members as they listened, at full, booming volume, to a tape of a man loudly emptying his bowels. They were roaring and cackling like apes and hyenas, portraying a great image for Thames Television Ltd..

Apart from the director and his immediate team, not that many people on the set, it seems to me, are 100% employed. Many are an over-staffed, overpaid union requirement. Three to do the job of one. (At least, that's how it used to be. Actually, the crew are now suffering from the same kind of cutbacks which are affecting us all.) True, the extras may not for the most part be overworked, but they don't **play** at being the 'workers'.

This attitude can also reflect in the eating arrangements; the 'crew first' syndrome, when we are ordered to wait while the entire produc-tion team are served with their food. It makes you feel like a social leper, which is how we are viewed. Fair enough, if the extras have been sitting about unused all morning and **some** of the crew have got to get straight back to work after one hour's break, but the system is often abused and the extras are deliberately humiliated and sometimes don't get their allotted time to eat. This breeds resentment on both sides.

Quite often, we noddies are not permitted to eat breakfast off of a plate. The rule, inexplicably, can be that the crew are allowed to have a full morning meal on brimming porcelain, whilst the extras can be chortled at as they try to balance egg, bacon, mushrooms, beans, etc., piled six inches high in a bread roll. This has always struck me as an insult and I can only guess at the reasoning behind it. Perhaps they think we're not safe handling anything with sharp edges.

I remember one chap taking particular exception. 'Why don't you just throw my food down on the ground,' he said, 'and I'll lap it up like a dog.'

The bottom line has got to be that we are all human. I would not for one moment suggest that all extras are saints, but the fact remains that too many elements on the production side generalise and assume that we are all from the same mould; i.e. anyone with any self respect would not allow themselves to be seen doing background work.

I see it like this. When you are self employed in showbusiness and try-ing to make a living, any area of work is fair game. Employment as an

extra is just another string to the bow, and let's face it, the productions couldn't be made without that background action. I know no end of people who might spend the day as a blurred shape passing the cafe window in EASTENDERS only to go on to an evening performing their own cabaret act. Or one of a mob of hundreds storming a castle might very well be in the West End next week playing a major role in a play. A lot of noddies even run their own businesses. Of course, there are those who earn their livings entirely from extra work and couldn't deliver a line if their lives depended upon it, but so what? Is that really any worse than working in an office or factory, or even on a film set, putting out props or erecting a lighting stand?

Much talk circulates in the noddy world regarding the desire for recognition. This is usually from the younger acting fraternity who go to great pains to tell you that they don't really do extra work, then will continue to be seen on calls for years to come. Then there are those who have become embittered and cynical and others who are critical of anyone who does manage to advance him or herself, but I suppose this is pure jealousy. I have often thought, if I ever did make it and walked through a crowd of extras, the ones who said, 'He never talks to us now' would be the ones I never spoke to anyway.

A final explanation of the term 'Noddy'. As an example, you may recall a now defunct soap opera about a Midland's motel. Customers at reception might be greeted with 'Here are your keys, sir. Your room is through that door on the right. Have a pleasant day'. If the customer replied it would cost the company money, so he just nods inanely. Hence 'Noddy'. It says it all.

STANDING IN

A small percentage of the film crowd make their livings almost entirely from standing in. These favoured few work virtually full time and go from film to film earning a fortune, but as they are on call just about permanently, I don't know when they get a chance to spend any of it. They are, to coin a phrase, well in. As far as I'm concerned, they're welcome to it.

I hate standing in. To me it is the most demeaning past-time in the whole business, yet, for some reason, several of the full time stand-ins tend to look down on the general crowd. It used to pay slightly more than a normal day but now it doesn't even do that. (Unless the stand-in has negotiated his/her own deal.) The best qualification is to be a crawler.

Standing in involves being on set in place of the main artistes, taking their positions and going through their action for initial lighting and rehearsal, thereby reducing the actual 'tedium time' that a principal will have to spend in front of the camera. In theory, stand-ins are supposed to be the same height, build and colouring as the artiste involved but in practice I have often seen balding fatties on the wrong side of fifty covering for young, virile types.

Competition for these jobs is fierce, politics being the number one consideration. After all, somebody with the right attitude stands to land weeks of work. A stand-in has to remain on hand at all times within finger flicking distance of the first assistant, ready to jump into position at a moment's notice. There is no time to skive or even relax as one is always supposed to know what is happening without being told. He/she is also supposed to 'look after' their artiste, getting them cups of tea, meals, etc.. It helps enormously to be naturally servile.

Some of the forced humility is nauseating to behold, perhaps because it has been known for big tips to be given at the end of a film's run. However, I couldn't help but laugh at the result one stand-in was awarded after weeks of bowing and scraping around a Hollywood star. He received a signed picture! (It puts me in mind of what Tommy Cooper would sometimes do when tipping an expectant hanger-on. 'Have a drink on me' he would say as he pressed a tea bag into their hand!)

There are a few stand-ins who, after long service, have actually become friends of the stars they have been involved with, but this is rare. Some have even been taken abroad to exotic locations and carry on their jobs to the extent of becoming a personal assistant; driving, arranging meetings, booking restaurant tables, etc.. One stand-in just couldn't keep up with his man's after work drinking sessions. Another stood in for Sean Bean on Ken Russell's LADY CHATTERLY and spent a few weeks indulging in simulated bonking.

I have only ever done one long running stand-in job. In spite of the fact that I made quite a lot of money, it was not a pleasant experience. On the second day of the shoot I had a run in with the first assistant. He told me my attitude was all wrong. I should show more interest in the filming. As far as I was concerned, I was always there when he wanted me and I did the job. The backside creeping he could forget.

'You're not an extra now,' he said, 'you're part of my team.'

This went down with me like a cast iron neck tie. When he went on to tell me that I was expected to help the third assistant stop traffic and keep people quiet during takes I had to draw the line.

'Why are you being so difficult?' he asked with a scowl.

'Because it's not my job,' I replied determinedly. As a coup-de-grace I added, 'You wouldn't ask a grips or sparks to do it.'

He missed my point entirely and wrote me off as an awkward son of a bitch. Since then it has actually become standard procedure for stand-ins to take on this 'role-play' as an assistant, but many of us find it sickening to see our ex-compatriots swanning around with walkie-talkies. Once they've got that aerialled black box in their hands a huge personality change comes over them.

Anyway, the assistant and I had a war of nerves for seven weeks and he delighted in putting me down whenever he could. I won't weep when he doesn't ask for me again.

There was another film stand-in job which could have been mine for the whole shoot but I cut myself (dropped out) on the third day because the other stand-in, an especially obnoxious example of the type I have been describing, tried her utmost to take control of me. Many people thought I was insane for blowing out all that money but there is only so much I can take. There comes a point where self respect takes precedence.

My other standing in experiences have been in the short term, I'm pleased to say. I have always particularly disliked having to get meals for the artistes. Very often the artistes themselves are embarrassed about it but the assistants invariably insist. I will always remember making up a ham salad for one actor only to discover later that he was Jewish.

TOP OF THE POPS was different. I didn't mind that as we were mostly left to ourselves and didn't have to act as servants. Also, it was interesting to see a bit a pop history in the making. Sting and Dire Straits when they were completely unknown and the Eurythmics when they were called the Tourists. Dramatic too. I remember when the lead vocalist of the Cockney Rejects (hit single; violent, punk rock version of 'I'm Forever Blowing Bubbles'!) wanted to stab all of the Lambrettas and had to be physically restrained by the floor manager. How showbusiness has changed since Noel Coward's day!

One day, whilst doing the Pops, three of us trooped up to the B.B.C. club for a drink and were stopped by a 'Jobsworth' at the door.

'Sorry lads. Got any I.D.?'

'It's okay. We're working on TOP OF THE POPS.'

'Oh yeh? Who are you then?'

'We're the stand-ins.'

He consulted his list and shook his head woefully. 'Nobody here of that name.'

He thought we were a band. The Standings! Or maybe the Stan Ding's!

Working on panel games or game shows is another experience. On the 1979 revival of JUKE BOX JURY I played everyone from Crystal Gale to Johnny Rotten. That was fun. In rehearsals we had to pass the same comments on the new releases that we thought the celebrities might make.

WHAT'S MY LINE, STRIKE IT LUCKY, FIFTEEN TO ONE ... there are so many. I had a nice run on the latter of these shows and ended up actually appearing on air as a contestant. (And doing far worse than I had ever done as a dummy contestant!) These sort of shows make a change and are usually nice, comfortable, easy days. Having said that, I can't say I was ever too keen on looking a prat on the GENERATION GAME, dressed as a Polish dancer or plate spinning. Mind you, ten of us had a good time on it once. Courtesy of Jim Davidson, we were able to regress to childhood fantasy when he wanted us to refight the battle of Culloden with custard pies! A glorious, juvenile mess was made by one and all. Now, it's not often in life that one gets paid to indulge in something like that!

I have had full prosthetic make-up jobs to enable me to double for people in certain situations, which is not that nice. I was Kenny Everett's double for a long time on his B.B.C. television series, as he used to do a lot of sketches where he played two parts and I would be required for 'over the shoulder' or distant shots. Another time I had to double for an actor in a commercial where I replaced him running in long shot up a down escalator. This was so that the poor devil wouldn't get too exhausted during the many takes they planned to do. However, the director decided that I didn't look enough like him and so the actor had to do the lot. I felt guilty because the unfortunate bloke actually got sick with fatigue.

On LITTLE SHOP OF HORRORS I doubled for Rick Moranis in the pre-production test shots when they were rehearsing with the man eating plant. It was incredible. A giant, mechanized monster, electronically operated by about a dozen puppeteers, each one responsible for individual tentacles and other bits. There was even a seperate controller for the tongue. When it sang to me, with faultless lip synchronisation, it seemed very real. Frankly, it was a bit terrifying!

HAIRCUTS

I stopped having make-up room haircuts a long time ago, around about the time when somebody told me I was beginning to resemble Bart Simpson. Once I would let them do anything to me, but then it dawned that I had a life to live in the outside world where attention might just be drawn to a scalped freak.

The trouble is, for some years now, the companies have been obsessed with making productuions set in the period between 1900 to 1960, when, they insist, everybody must have spent their lives in the barber's chair. The make-up girls, for the most part, are hardly top stylists. They try, but usually they are not concerned with the way you look as long as it is acceptable on screen, taking the line that the extras, as they are getting paid, should accept anything. We are accused of being unprofessional if we complain about the thirty nine steps up the back of our necks. Then they leave it all thick on top and clippered up the sides so that you look like a windswept thistle. Once, when I objected to this image, I was told I looked trendy, 'like one of the Fun Boy Three'! Then, very often, wardrobe will give you something to wear like a balaclava helmet so that the whole stupid aggravation has been in vain.

It is also annoying when principal artistes are seen with their hair in modern styles. 'Artistic prerogative' we are told. Tell that to the historical advisor. There have been times when people have been asked to have their heads totally shaved and this can be financially rewarding. So it should be. Personally, they would have to give me the deeds to Buckingham Palace at least, but there are individuals who have gladly let them run amok with the shears for a few bob.

A good deal arose for those who played the bald priests on a B.B.C. series set in ancient Egypt. Weeks of work, a large bonus plus a wig. Not bad, I suppose, although one man regretted it when his hair grew back like pubic fluff. Driving home one night with another shaven priest, they were stopped by the police and arrested on suspicion as car stealing skinheads.

Another fellow was completely shaven for a couple of day's work on a film about Hitler's S.S., a Disney production, no doubt. He was the type of chap who would have allowed them to infect him with typhoid for an extra fiver. Unfortunately, he turned up on another job for which he had been booked before his de-hairing. To his horror he was told that they couldn't use a bald man but, undaunted, he went away and returned a short time later with a hairstyle **painted** on his head!

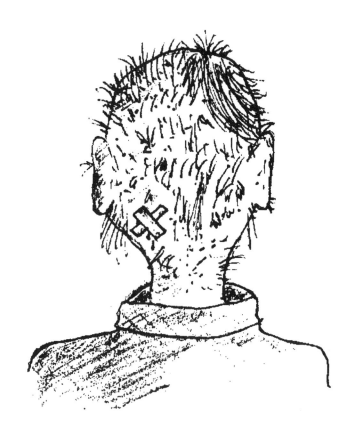

THE B.B.C. HAIRCUT

IDENTITY PARADE

One fine day an agent asked me if I minded appearing on an identity parade. Why not? I had done plenty of these before in a host of detective programmes, but this one was for real. It turned out to be a police experiment, to use actors on video in place of a live I.D. parade. There was a reason for this as we were soon to find out.

A dozen of us assembled at the police section house behind Lambeth magistrate's court and were met in a bare room by a pair of Flying Squad sergeants and an Inspector. A video tape recorder and monitor were wheeled in and the explanation commenced.

It seemed that a particularly nasty piece of work was in police custody. Over a two year period this man had shot nineteen people in the course of armed robberies, three of them being policemen. (One of whom had been crippled for life.) The robber, according to estimates, had netted hundreds of thousands of pounds, very little of which they had been able to recover. He liked shooting people, usually in the legs, just for the hell of it, and would even find a victim **after** he had got his spoils. Once he had tried to blast his way through the armoured glass of a security van just to get at the guard out of spite. Delightful chap.

The Flying Squad had caught him after an underworld tip off. Surrounding his hide out with armed officers, they burst in and had him in cuffs before he could reach the loaded pistol he had at his side. Now it seemed he was refusing to co-operate and wouldn't appear on any identity parades. Apparently there was enough evidence to convict him anyway but the police just wanted something to 'ice the cake'. So, they decided to film him in secret arriving at court, and then use actors to copy his actions as seen on screen. The bogus tapes would then be mixed with the real thing and shown to the witnesses.

We viewed the actual man on tape and could see straightaway that he was capable of all he had been accused of. Then we had to impersonate him. It didn't take long and it made an interesting morning talking to the detectives about their work. Straight from the SWEENEY. I thought no more about it until about four months later when the case came up in the national press. Something like 'Mad Dog Gets Life!' Yes, it was him alright. I shall call him John Coonan.

Whilst on remand in Brixton prison he had greased his naked body with baby oil before going berserk with an iron bar. Slippery as an eel, he put two warders in hospital before they managed to subdue him. Now he had been sentenced to twenty five years to give him time to reflect.

The story does not end there...

A short time after this, I was working on a commercial and was telling this tale to a group of associates. One or two strangers were listening and I was going on about what a nasty bastard Mr. Coonan must be. Suddenly one of the guys I didn't know (he was a featured artiste playing a football fan) said to me, 'I know who you're talking about. John Coonan.' His brow furrowed and his voice hardened. 'He's one of my best mates.'

I froze and was struck speechless. Would you believe it? Of all the people to open my big mouth in front of. I waffled on matily as he mumbled, 'You shouldn't have done that job,' and such like. My previous audience were finding it hard to suppress their hilarity.

'Knew him well, eh?' I gulped, frantically trying to play it down.

'Since school. We called him 'Dirty Harry' Coonan.'

'Oh? Why's that?'

'Cos he always carried two forty fives. Johnny Coonan's a good bloke. All he did was shoot coppers. He's a victim of circumstances.'

'What about **his** victims then?' sneered some smart arse.

'He's a good bloke,' persisted our friend. Then to me, 'You shouldn't have done that job.'

My first thought was that in twenty five years I should consider changing my identity.

STRONG STOMACHS

I have had to do some pretty repulsive things in the name of 'art'. A group of us portraying medical students in a television play about Keats the poet had to watch a man having his leg sawn off without anaesthetic. Very realistic it was too.

Many's the time we have had to eat in studio canteens covered in the scars of battle. Once, when I was alone in the B.B.C. watering hole, blood seeping from my synthetic wounds as I munched my lunch, I couldn't help overhearing some secretaries at the next table voicing their objections rather loudly. 'God, can't they find some other place to feed them?' I suppose they had a point.

My brother spent weeks on end as a psoriasis victim on THE SINGING DETECTIVE, spending ages in make-up each morning having flakey flesh stuck on. Yuk!

He and I had the honour of being picked for a medical training video to show different methods of dealing with battle wounds past and present, and showing how they compare with modern day road accident victims. Have you ever thought over the similarity of getting skewered by a twelfth century spearsman and finding yourself impaled on the railings at the local park? No? Then how about the fact that getting hit by a car at thirty miles per hour is just like being run down by an armour clad knight's charger?

I had to have a section of false leg fitted at one stage which, when pressed, squirted pus and blood in several directions. Ingenious really. That make-up man certainly knew his job. It can be quite fascinating to watch as long as you are not planning to eat for a while.

On another programme, I was cast as a zookeeper who is killed by a frenzied giraffe. For this they covered me from head to toe in giraffe crap, the real article which they had scooped from the bottom of the killer's pen (we were filming in London Zoo), and painted bloody hoof prints all over me. The caterers wouldn't let me anywhere near their wagon (not that I had much of an appetite!) and when I went out to make a telephone call I caused quite a sensation. Did I really put up with that? My stomach has usually been able to take this kind of thing. What makes it do triple somersaults is when I observe certain

Batteries damp ..
my horns won't
light up ...
No wonder I look
unhappy!
'BLAKES SEVEN"
(B.B.C.)

I look slightly
happier here,
having just been
killed by a
giraffe in
"OLD MEN AT
THE ZOO"
(B.B.C.)

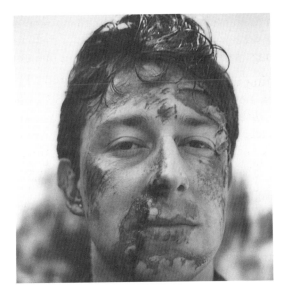

stand-ins in action.

A friend of mine worked on MONTY PYTHON'S MEANING OF LIFE film which, by all accounts, was a pretty unpleasant experience. He was in the scene where a grotesque, fat man in a restaurant keeps on eating until he starts to throw up before eventually exploding, showering the other diners in entrails and vomit. Tasteful stuff. This exquisite tableau took several days to shoot, during which time they were using the same vats of stale vegetable soup and other dross which they had concocted to pass for the required gunge. Apparently the stench was beyond belief.

Working on BETWEEN THE LINES, I was chatting to one of the bogus policemen. He was quite a serious type who was telling me intensely that he was about to give up extra work to go to college. Suddenly, he hesitated in mid sentence and a look of unbridled horror flickered across his face. I thought at first that he was having an attack of some sort but slowly he drew his hand from the pocket of his uniform trousers and gingerly opened his palm. There, gleaming in the sunlight, was a complete top set of false teeth! Well, as you can imagine, this brought the house down, but it was topped by the fact that a moment later his face grew even paler as he drew from the other pocket the full bottom set! Wardrobe were totally baffled. Whoever it was who had previously worn this costume, how the hell had he managed to go home without missing his teeth?

Getting back to the subject of toleration, I must mention the longest week I ever spent when I worked on a German business training film. The director, the entire cast and most of the crew were German, as was all the dialogue, and I spoke about as much of the language as Jack Duckworth. The director was a pure caricature. Think of all those old war films with Nazi commandants, sprinkle in a touch of Erich von Stroheim and the Marquis de Sade and you will have a fair picture of him. He spent the week gesturing and strutting about, forgetting totally that I did not speak his language. Consequently, I missed a few cues and cocked up a few times. Plus, it did not help that the whole thing was mind mincingly boring, all about sales figures and percentages with the set consisting of table, chairs and a blackboard. What chance did I have? I didn't know my donner und blitzen from my strudel.

The final straw came when Attila the Hun screamed at me, 'Vy must you mek like you are stu-pit?'

I wouldn't swallow that kind of treatment now, but then age and experience has made me less tolerant and less afraid of tyrants.

My brother and I
acting "butch" for a
medical training
video at
Bisley Firing Range
– Ray drew the short
straw!

DIRECTORS

Some directors are very charming, and though deep down you know that they are probably regarding you as being on the same level as a dried bogey, it's still much better to be spoken to like a human being whether it's sincere or not. On big productions, there is not usually much contact between the director and the extras and his instructions are relayed via the first assistant. This was taken to ridiculous extremes on a famous television soap opera on which I had been fortunate enough to be given a line.

The director was a vile woman who had a great deal of power in the company as she was also the producer and brainchild behind the series. She was truly awful. Everyone was terrified of her, even the principals, and it made a most miserable atmosphere on the set. I had to smile when I heard her interviewed on the radio and she said her production was like one big happy family. Any of her cast or team could come to her for advice, she said. And be executed for their trouble, thought I.

She wouldn't speak to me, even though I and another Walk-On were the only two people involved in the shot. In spite of the fact that I was standing right next to her, every order for me was given to the production manager who then had to repeat it for my benefit. Having got through this dreadfully strained episode and I had uttered about half a dozen interpretations of my precious line, she turned away and snarled, 'Right, now let's do something with the actors.'

Nasty bitch. It was so pointed even some of the crew winced.

A few months later I was on the same production as 'man with dog'. My pooch, bless him, must have instinctively felt for me because he ended up in a savage fight with her dog, a big, poncy poodle which was something of a celebrity on the show in its own right. Not much of a revenge but kind of symbolic, I thought.

Another director famous for his 'charm' was an American who ran his own very successful company filming commercials. He had won many awards and, I must confess, has turned out some good stuff. It's just a shame that he was such a pig to work with. Short and wizened with a pronounced Bronx accent, he was incapable of speaking in a calm manner. Everything would be screamed at fever pitch and even the crew were not safe from his wrath. He always worked as if the pressure was really on and therefore created terrible tension. Perhaps he thought that this was the best way to obtain results. Anyway, he was so fearsome that very often, first thing in the morning before the shoot had begun, the assistant would gather everyone together and warn them what to expect. He was a twenty five carat bastard and I often imagined him being henpecked at home.

I once saw him reduce a girl to tears when he grabbed her by the shoulders to bawl her out. Another time he threw a man off the set because the poor fool had dared to enquire what time they were going to finish. On another occasion somebody failed to turn up for the second day's filming because they were laid up in hospital with food poisoning.

'What?!' screamed the American Dream, 'I'll give the mother food poisoning! I'll see he never works again!'

A pianist friend of mine was featured in one of his commercials, to be seen in just one shot, seated in close up at the piano as a bottle of sherry slides past him. The shot took hours to set up for some reason and during the day this pianist, being dark haired and rugged, developed a bit of five o'clock shadow on his chin.

'Hey!' roared our lovely director, 'What's that shit on your face?!'

'Oh, I probably need another shave.'

'Shave in your time not mine!'

'But I...'

'Move your ass and have one, goddam klutz!'

As my friend sloped away, the bastard added, within everyone's earshot, 'Jeez-us! What a nothing face!'

I was on a beer commercial for him where we were supposed to be playing bowls. The weather had been glorious all morning as he ranted and raved, walkie-talkie in one hand, megaphone in the other. He probably had a six gun concealed in his jacket too. Briefly, a patch of cloud went across the sun, daring to delay him.

Fuming, he glowered at the sky. 'Okay God,' he growled, waving a fist at Heaven, 'cut the crap!'

For one wonderful moment I thought he may get frazzled by a thunderbolt.

There is another very well known British director of feature films who is infamous for his behaviour. He is so notorious that I am sure he actually finds it necessary to play up to his image, although on chat shows he insists that his reputation has only arisen from his being a perfectionist who will take no nonsense. This in itself is nonsense as one only has to see the man to recognise that he is on a permanent ego trip.

He looks not unlike a snake eyed toad. Also, he has (or had) his own slave, a pathetic young chap whose role in life appeared to be to jump to the toad's every whim. This slave had to follow him at all times around the set, always two paces in his shadow, constantly alert to snaps of the fingers. One snap might mean, 'Pass me the script', two snaps 'Light my cigar' and so on. He has turned belittling people into an art form.

Many of his films have been filled with nudity and violence and he is a great campaigner in saying that such crassness, for its own sake, is harmless fun. To be fair, I think that a few of his films have been entertaining, but he is certainly no celluloid genius and he does seem preoccupied with scenes of bloody mayhem and sexual humiliation. He brushes aside all critiscism with his usual smugness, saying he is only giving the public what they want. This, of course, is an issue in itself and perhaps is a sad indictment of our society. I am sure a huge mass of the population would approve of public hangings too but that doesn't make it right. For a long time he had a very public affair with a much younger, well known actress who regularly insisted that he was a lovely man, but then I suppose she would say that. The poor souls who work for him can only make a character assessment at face value.

He champions many causes, always, seemingly, in a blaze of publicity. There are numerous stories of his brutal, uncalled for rudeness, particularly to the extras who he apparently detests. There is a tale which tells of how he could not get the shock horror reaction he wanted from a crowd. Exasperated, he called a tea break, had the urn laced with explosives, then blew it up, thus filming the expressions he wanted. Shrewd if drastic!

Another story in circulation, which I am sure cannot be true, is worth relating anyway as it is so representative of the kind of man he is. Apparently, he wanted to seperate a crowd into two groups and was addressing them in his inimitable way.

'Right then, listen! So that there is no confusion, you lot over there will be known as the arseholes and you lot are the c...s.'

One man objected strongly to this. 'Do you mind? I am not a c...!'

'Get over there with the arseholes then!'

Another version has it that when someone showed confusion as to which group they belonged, the response was, 'You're an arsehole, you c...!'

An extra I knew (who has since become an agent) deserves mention here for a wonderful retort he made to the toad. Wardrobe had dressed our man up in an outsize trenchcoat and trilby and when the toad saw him he sniped, 'Good God, you look like something out of a B movie.'

'Well,' quipped the extra, quick as a flash, 'you keep making 'em and I'll keep appearing in 'em!'

Actually, these days this director seems to spend more of his time writing a regular column for one of the seamier tabloid newspapers and is showing signs of mellowing. Hope for us all, I guess.

When I look back it is with the realisation that I have been directed by some of the biggest names in the business. David Bailey (what a pseudo scruff **he** is), Don Siegel, John Schlesinger, Andrew McClagen, Ridley Scott... and they all ignored me! However, it was hard for Alan Parker to ignore me. I havn't worked on any of his films but as a solo performer I was booked to perform at a small private dinner party at Groucho's Club where he was a guest. More recently, the same booker, a casting director who seems to like us, booked my partner and I to play at her birthday party. It was a small affair again but once more Mr. Parker was in attendance, looking somewhat the worse for wear after a day of meetings regarding the impending release of EVITA. Even so we had him dancing on his chair. What a party that was. We ended up accompanying the surviving guests from the restaurant round to the

"NELSON" (A.T.V.)
With Colin Cook who, apparently, was once a big name
in Australian Rock Music. How the mighty can fall .....

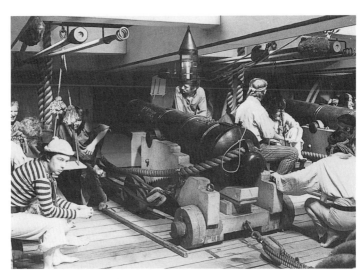

**Contemplating the Battle of Trafalgar
in Studio One at Elstree.**

casting director's house where we carried on playing until almost four in the morning. (I must be honest. I wouldn't have been so accommodating for the concert secretary of the Willesden Working Man's Club!)

Speaking of Ridley Scott, I witnessed a gem of an incident involving him. Now, being the director of such atmospheric pieces as ALIEN, BLADERUNNER, THE DUELLISTS, 1492, etc., (not to mention the Hovis commercials!) Mr. Scott has a fine reputation. He is also renowned for being extremely pernickety when setting up his shots, hence working for him is a slow and tedious business. On a rare break from his feature film career, he was making a Coca Cola commercial starring Whitney Houston and quite a few of us from the G2 agency. No prizes for guessing who got top billing.

The scene was supposed to portray a packed rock concert and a couple of us were dressed in white coats and placed behind a counter as vendors. We were quite excited by this as it looked like a feature might be in the air. The vendor with me was a spikey haired, North country lad by the name of Lee. He was a bit of a joker and his eyes rested on a target. Ridley Scott, doing his own camera work, was seated in a wheelchair so that he could get a low angle tracking shot. Needless to say, his minions were fussing around him as they endlessly rolled him up and down amidst a tangle of lights, cables and instructions.

'Excuse me,' piped up Lee, pleasantly, interrupting the great man's artistic flow, 'are you Raymond Burr?'

The atmosphere froze as everyone glared at Lee in disbelief. Ridley Scott didn't utter a word but the assistant hissed, 'Got another job to go to have you?'

Lee just couldn't see what all the fuss was about. 'Who the hell's Ridley Scott?' he asked me afterwards. And quite right too. These film people take themselves far too seriously.

I have been directed by Jonathan Miller on a couple of occasions, and though intense, he is really a very nice man. His method of working is to involve everybody, no matter how small their role. Consequently, it tends to phase you a bit if you are playing fifth spearsman on the left and he suddenly approaches you to ask your opinion. He was directing one of the B.B.C. Shakespeare productions and after several days rehearsal, he gathered his cast and extras together for a final briefing before the recording. Amongst the crowd was a character named Tom who had recently started his own sideline in the form of an office cleaning business. Bored with the Bard, Tom's mind was elsewhere as his eyes wandered around the large, grubby rehearsal room.

'It's our first day in the studio tomorrow,' beamed Mr. Miller, with all the enthusiasm of a gym mistress on a school day trip, 'so has anybody got any questions?'

'Yeh,' said Tom, 'who cleans this gaff?'

The acclaimed writer/director Stephen Poliakoff is a strange one. Physically resembling a cross between Rasputin and Ken Dodd, his manner of working is eccentric to the point of lunacy. I had a couple of nightcalls on his film CENTURY, an Edwardian piece which we shot in freezing, rainy conditions. It was supposed to be a summer garden party so we were all garbed in evening dress and told to act jolly. We were also wearing a bizarre variety of animal masks. I was an eagle and I was put in a position in front of the bandstand with a man dressed as a jester. Poliakoff was filming some cutaways so he singled us out and asked the jester what he intended to do in the shot.

'You would dance and act the fool, wouldn't you?' he suggested.

The jester nodded but that wasn't good enough for Poliakoff. 'Show me,' he insisted.

And so, the poor red faced jester had to make a complete tit of himself, leaping, cackling and twirling to the delight of the assembled crowd and crew. I must admit, I was secretly enjoying his misery, chuckling behind my mask, when Poliakoff spoke again, saying, 'And you...eagle! What will **you** be doing?'

I am told that the show the jester and the eagle put on on that wet shivery night almost made up for the discomfort.

One more director story, and this is one of my favourites. Six midgets were needed, at short notice (no pun intended!), and having got them, the director gathered them into a small group (sorry!) to explain what he wanted.

'Okay, the shot is like this. You two midgets come tumbling in from the left and you two come tumbling in from the right. And you two little guys, I want an extra special tumble from you right down the middle...'

The midgets stared blankly at one another. 'Er...' said the midget spokesman, nervously, 'we don't tumble.'

The director blinked and glared back at them. 'What, none of you?'

'None of us.'

Completely at a loss, the director slumped back into his chair, scratching his head and saying, 'Christ, what's the point of being a midget if you don't tumble?'

NUDITY

Nudity has reared its spotty behind on a few occasions in my chequered career, although I have only succumbed once. Yes, I confess. I was conned into baring my all, prostituting my talent for mere profit, and not much profit at that.

The telephone rang and an agent breezily asked, 'Would you object to showing your bottom?'

I assumed that this was an offer of work and it transpired that the honour had first been offered to my brother who had got cold feet (or something) and had suggested me. Well, I wasn't keen. I had once been to an audition for something like this and had missed it by an inch! (Only kidding!) The agent was insistent and I got the impression she was having trouble finding people.

'Oh, go on. It'll be a giggle. It's for the Spike Milligan show. Six of you as policemen on a closed set. All you've got to do is drop your trousers for a moment. Over in a flash, and there's an extra fee.'

I felt like a whore but reluctantly agreed to do it. She breathed a huge sigh of relief and I began to regret it immediately. When the big day came, I was called for the crack of dawn at the B.B.C. television centre where my five sheepish comrades were waiting. I didn't know any of them and these were the days when you knew nearly everybody in the game, at least by sight. God only knows where this bunch had sprung from. As we waited for our transport out to Pinewood studios, we gradually broke the ice; 'Are you showing your arse too?' etc., and were soon complaining and making excuses to one another. 'I'm only doing this as a favour...' and so on. What a set of weirdos we must have appeared. At Pinewood we were shown to a wardrobe truck and greeted by one of the gayest dressers I have ever met. (And that's saying something!) 'Ooooh, come on, boys, let's have a look at you then!'

I should have known. We had to strip off entirely and were garbed only in policemen's helmets, boots and truncheons! They only had four dressing gowns for us to wear inbetween takes so the other two had to make do with dirty macs. No closed set either. We were on the back lot in the open, waist high in stinging nettles as buses passed by. The crew seemed to have expanded with more make-up girls than usual, poised sniggering with their polaroids and comparing notes.

The scene was this. We were supposed to be the vice squad. A police van (containing us) comes screeching into a clearing and we pile out and line up at attention, truncheons poised. A sergeant barks, 'Right lads, into the woods and watch out for woodpeckers!' and we trot away stage left. All simple family hokum. Our dressing gowns and macs were taken away and we sat alongside each other in the back of the van. Milligan popped his head in and in that inimitable Eccles' voice enquired, 'Who's that with two truncheons?'

The driver was a lunatic. He overdid the skidding and we were thrown all over the place. I got some alien genitalia in my ear. The door burst open and out we leaped to line up as told. Over comes the director.

'Okay chaps. No full frontals. This is the B.B.C.!'

I keep thinking that this one is going to come back and haunt me one day.

Several of the agents had a brief to find twenty people willing to be naked and painted green, lying on mortuary slabs with water dripping onto them. I declined. On a lighter note, there was the man who stripped, save for a tiny pouch, for an historical drama. With nowhere to put his watch, he tucked it away inside his pouch. Unfortunately, halfway through a take, the alarm activated and his privates began to go 'Peep, peep, peep'!

There have been orgy scenes for various films but I have never been involved. The real surprise comes when one finds out which individuals actually let it all hang out. Often they are the least likely, and with some of the bodies they offer, one wonders why they were accepted or how they had the gall.

In one debauched scene in THE BORGIAS, one reveller couldn't believe his luck when a topless wench was placed on his lap and he was told to cavort with her. (Seventy five pounds for the day. Not a lot but it was all he could afford!) Real wine was served and the wench got somewhat inebriated. Before the fun really got going she threw up all over him.

Once or twice, I have been in things where we were supposed to be an audience in a strip club. No matter how good the girl is at her routine, after a repetitive morning under the lights everyone's interest begins to wane. And then it's lunch. Every extra's highlight of the day!

EXTRA TYPES

MISTAKEN IDENTITY

I underwent an unfortunate case of mistaken identity whilst playing a Castrovalvan warrior in DOCTOR WHO. We were garbed in identical skin tight outfits of a pastel shade, complete with constrictive hoods. Like decorative condoms. Once we had our deathly white make-up on it was very difficult to tell us apart.

Lounging around in the green room inbetween scenes, drinking endless cups of coffee, as is an extra's wont, I was idling away the time with an aquaintance who I shall call Frank. Now, Frank was not an over educated lad. He was, as is known in the trade, a bit rough, and would turn up on jobs driving a horse box. When asked how he got his Equity card he would grow restless and mumble something about being on the stage. Pressed for details about what he did he would mumble, 'Jokes n' songs n' that'.

I was sitting with my feet up, counting the cracks in the ceiling, and Frank had his copy of The Sun spread out on the table in front of him. A cleaner was doing his rounds wiping the tables when he accidentally knocked Frank's coffee all over his newspaper. Being an excitable sort, Frank launched straight in with a torrent of abuse at the bemused cleaner who was not exactly a potential MENSA candidate himself. Not given a chance to apologise, the cleaner, who was broad Irish, spat back with a verbal attack of his own. It blew over pretty quickly and after a few insults had been exchanged, the cleaner moved on, making his final exit with a snarled over the shoulder threat.

'Bollocks!' snapped back Frank, venomously.

It had served as a mildly interesting diversion and that, we thought, was that.

Several hours later, the day's recording over, we were waiting for a clear. My fellow Castrovalvans were in the dressing room but I was still in the green room talking to one of the dressers. Suddenly, our Irish cleaner friend reappeared, this time with some support, equally Irish and equally drunk. The pair approached me and the cleaner, somewhat unsteady on his feet, said, 'So there yez are!'

I looked at him, puzzled.

'Arrr...' he growled, 'not so brave now, are yez?'

I asked him what he was going on about as he laughed and drooled like a maniac. 'Forgotten this mornin' have we, boyo? Not so much to say without yez friends around, eh? All in ye' pretty dresses, ye' great jessies!' He pulled at the sleeve of my costume and put his fists up. 'Come on, we've got t'ings t' settle!'

An horrendous predicament, innocent as I was. I suppose, after ten pints of Guinness, all Castrovalvan warriors must look the same. A nightmare vision swam into view of me involved in undignified combat with this nutcase. Banned from the B.B.C. for brawling. Oh, the shame! The dresser, camp as a row of tents, raised his hands in horror and fled.

Well, I am pleased to report that it never came to blows, thanks to some swift diplomacy on my part, but the Finian pugilist never believed that he had confronted the wrong man. He and his pal went away convinced that I had backed down. Frank thought the whole thing hilarious. I expect he put it in his act, whatever that was.

Speaking of recognition, a funny thing happened to me in my local Chinese takeaway shop. I was a regular there, but the management had no idea what I did for a living. At the time, there was a commercial running for London Transport in which I was quite heavily featured. As I leaned on the counter, awaiting my order and idly watching the television, this commercial came on. The Chinese serving girl did a double take from the T.V. set to me, then, pointing, she asked, 'Tha' you?'

I nodded sheepishly and she grinned like a fiend. Turning on her heel, she dashed into the kitchen jabbering a cacophony of oriental rhetoric. Within seconds the whole family had appeared to view me, two beaming faces at the hatch, a few more at the door, granny and all.

I still had to pay for the food though.

EXTRA
TRYING TO
EAT WHILST
WEARING A
FALSE BEARD

WORST JOBS

There are many reasons for jobs being considered bad and I can think of several candidates which merit proposal as the worst. Sometimes it is just the boredom. Repetitive retakes can drive one to the brink of insanity. One of the least happy experiences is to turn up on a very early call to find that your fellow extras are all people you cannot stand, you have forgotten to bring a book to read and the day looms ahead like a prison sentence. At times like this, after a twelve hour day, one can actually sink into a kind of comatose state.

Another reason is the cold. There is little worse than being stuck for hours on end on some forlorn, windswept location, usually dressed in some inadequate costume, with the temperature at sub zero. I remember once we had to work all through one winter's night in shirt sleeves. 'Think warm,' smirked the assistant as he snuggled into his capoc jacket.

Top of the list for bizarre and demeaning jobs must surely go to a promotion I was involved in for Volvo cars. At each of the main line London railway stations, six of us were required to wear large sandwich boards with 'The End of the World is Nigh' emblazoned on them. We then had to walk about amidst the teaming crowds during the height of the rush hour. The idea was that we would return to catch the same crowds during the evening rush, this time with sandwich boards which said 'Don't You Wish Everything Was As Reliable As A Volvo?' This was to be followed up with a television campaign. You can just imagine the smugness of the bright spark who dreamed that one up down at the advertising agency.

The problem was, the logistics had not been thought through properly. Initially, during the morning session, the harrassed commuters thought we were for real and we were either ignored, dragged into philosophical arguments or verbally abused. By and large we were regarded as an enormous nuisance, especially by the British Rail authorities and Transport police who were far from amused. They demanded to know by what authority we were traipsing around on private property. Eventually we were told to leave or we would be arrested for trespassing and causing public disorder. (At one of the stations, I'm told that the group were actually taken into custody.) The evening session was even more chaotic and short lived. By and large the whole thing was a disaster.

I had the dubious honour, along with several hundred other wretched souls, of being employed on yet another remake of the Robin Hood legend, PRINCE OF THIEVES. Though a big budget Hollywood picture, very little of the cash, by film standards, came our way. The star, Kevin Costner, was on an absolute fortune and the sets were magnificent, yet the producers had negotiated a deal with Central Casting which removed many of our usual perks. In other words, no payment for 'special action', the magic phrase which so often made film work lucrative. To my knowledge, this was the first time such a deal had been struck and it set a precedent, as will be seen.

They chose to shoot in the winter, usually on the back lot at Shepperton (City of Nottingham set) or in the depths of Burnham Beeches (Sherwood Forest set). True to say, there was plenty of work on it, weeks on end without a break for some people (they looked like zombies) but, by God, did we feel that we had earned the money.

The average call time was 6.30am. when along with two, three or four hundred others, one would join the first of the day's many endless queues. Having collected your chit, the next queue would be to pick up your costume and have your chit stamped 'Wardrobe Issued' (just in case you were thinking of absconding with a pile of rags) then, after a free for all fight for space in the marquee to get the gear on, it would be over to the make-up rooms where grumpy, overworked girls would roughly smear us with grime. One blessing arose in that it was possible to wear your own clothes under the costume's robes, which saved a lot of time at the end of the day. Also, the lucky ones had hoods. Those without would have to join another queue for a wig. The next queue would be for the coffee and tea urns, then a rushed breakfast before the assistants would come around like shepherds ushering everyone onto the set just as the sun was rising, so as to make the most of the day's available light.

The Shepperton set was ankle deep in mud and livestock crap and after the first day, it was quickly sussed that a piece of necessary apparel would have to be plastic carrier bags worn over two pairs of thick socks and your own shoes. This insulated the feet and made them waterproof, a great necessity as the period overshoes they issued were totally useless and were soon dragging behind your legs like sodden sandbags.

Once on the set, the secret was to find yourself a secluded nook or cranny so that you could keep well out of the way, otherwise you would be constantly used in scenes of mayhem. Normally, one might try to get in on this action and thus earn extra cash, but on this extravaganza there was no chance of pulling in one solitary bean over the top. The production people were very adamant about that. A lot of non-union bodies were used too (another precedent), many of whom went completely loopy when weapons were placed in their hands. There were several quite nasty injuries. Horses galloping about, missiles flying, mud squelching, skirmishes raging, goats and sheep shitting, assistants shouting... oh yes, it all made for a pleasant day out, ha, ha!

During a hanging scene we were told to pelt the victims with mouldy bread but certain idiots began throwing turnips. Have you ever been struck by a speeding turnip? It's not much fun, I can tell you.

We were constantly being moaned at for not showing enough enthusiasm! For what they were paying us, apathy was the most they should have expected. It was false economy. Pay people what they are due and they will act accordingly. Satisfied with a good financial result, the extras will work happily, creating a good vibe on set which results in a better end product for one and all. Cutting corners never seems to work.

Morning coffee break became the next queue, but if you were any further than half way back you would be very lucky if you actually got any. Lunch (another melee which passed for a queue) would often be taken 'on the run' and the moment you had swallowed your last morsel you would be forced back into the mud for filming to resume.

At least you knew they had to finish at the same time each day as the light faded. As that time drew near, there would be a great surging movement in the direction of the wardrobe tents, then, as the assistant shouted 'That's a wrap!', there followed a scene reminiscent of the California gold rush. Many were trampled in the carnage that ensued as hundreds of desperate, frozen, muddied extras fought to remove their costumes, hand them in, scrape off their make-up and be first in the paying off queue. Tempers wore very thin during these mad scrambles and rows broke out as the mob pushed, shoved and bickered. Dignity became a dirty word as animal instinct took over, the one driving desire being to get away from this asylum at any cost. To make matters worse, some of the extras, in costume, were acting as unofficial stewards. In many cases, this had gone to their heads and they were relishing the power of being able to order people about. It caused much bad feeling.

The day's money usually included two to three hours overtime to cover the early call and broken lunch, plus perhaps an hour to cover getting changed and queueing. Many held back or went to the bar as those at the end of the queue were usually paid for the inconvenience of waiting. However, most of the crowd couldn't wait to get away and so the fights would rage on in the line as the jibbers tried to push their way in. The excuses were varied but always pathetic. 'I'm giving him a lift', 'I've just got to give someone a message' or 'let me in…I'm collecting the money for an old man who can't breathe'. Either that or they would just openly stand in front of you, glaring with contempt and daring you to protest. Others tried to be more subtle, standing at the side of the queue looking thoughtful before sidling in, but it amounted to the same thing. These people are professional, ignorant, selfish pigs. It is really not worth getting involved in disputes with them.

I worked on PRINCE OF THIEVES (I think it was the producer's life story) for several days here and there, but never for more than three at a time. Frankly, it was about all I could physically take before going on to other more civilized calls that I had been previously booked on. It made every other job seem luxurious. As I signed off and the assistant said, 'Same time tomorrow', it gave me a warm glow to be able to say, 'Sorry, I'm not available'.

One day I was reprieved by a day's work on a nice cosy commercial for good money, which by coincidence was shooting on the sound stage right next to the Robin Hood set. I'm afraid I couldn't resist going round for a little gloat at my suffering compatriots, even though two days later I was back with them as if I had never been away. One seasoned extra was heard to say, 'I thought he only robbed from the rich'. The production came to be known as Robbin' Bastards.

A few years later I thought I was going through a bout of deja vu when I was back at Shepperton for what initially looked like a repeat performance. The film FIRST KNIGHT was another mediaeval epic which ran for weeks, but this time conditions were much better. This production really had its act together, and though there were yet again hundreds of us milling about a massive set, the whole thing was very well organized. Queues moved quickly, facilities were clean, the heaters were efficient and generally everything ran like clockwork. For a big call it went very smoothly, showing that it can be done if they put their minds to it. The stars were Richard Gere and Sean Connery, both of whom I saw subjected to examples of the more tiresome aspects of noddydom; the kind of thing that blackens the reputation of us all. It being well known that Richard Gere is a keen follower of Buddhism, I couldn't believe one stupid woman's crass attempt to draw his attention to her when she followed him about the set very openly (and un-naturally) clutching a book on the subject. I was delighted that he didn't give her the satisfaction of responding to such clumsy tactics. Sean Connery was actually half way through his dialogue on a long take when some idiot's mobile phone started ringing. This caused pandemonium as herds of panicky assistants rushed into the crowd, demanding that everybody immediately surrender their phones. These things really have become a problem on film sets as there always seems to be someone who forgets to switch theirs off. As for Mr. Connery, he remained stoical, but you got the impression that you wouldn't like to see his reaction if it happened a second time.

There have been many awful jobs, but if I had to pick one to serve as the prime example of film hell on earth...

It was a pilot show for a major series about the Kings and Queens of England. As far as I know, it was never shown and never got beyond the making of the first episode. (Probably because the cast didn't survive the experience.) The initial tale dealt with the reign of William the Conqueror and the troubles he had with the Saxon rebels under Hereward the Wake. Droves of bodies were employed to make up the ranks for the numerous crowd and battle scenes, and they decided to film it in the middle of one of the bitterest Januaries in living memory.

By the coachload they would transport us to the heart of the countryside where we were dressed as Saxons or Normans. It was best to be the latter, if you could swing it, because at least then you didn't

'FIRST KNIGHT' When's lunch?

My duo partner,
MARTYN ORAM,
trying to look
taller than me!

have to suffer a full matted wig and a massive beard cemented to your face, so that when you ate, it was like consuming the contents of a burst mattress. Huddled around an inefficient heater in some deserted farmhouse, we waited in dread of being called out to the location. Thermal underwear did little to stave off the cold and some of us even had to wear wet suits under our costumes. This was so that, once the ice had been broken, we could wade waist deep across a river!

I lost count of the number of battles I fought, with real weapons too. (Although these weapons were blunted, it was still possible to be split asunder when faced in combat by some clumsy lunatic.) They even had a bunch of us on top of a tower, swiping away at a crazed mob of stuntmen as they swarmed over the parapet. I got a whack on the head from an axe which drove the rim of my helmet into the bridge of my nose. As the blood ran down my face, they must have made quite a saving on make-up, yet they wouldn't even grant us a Walk-On.

At one point, three of us were selected to play sentinels on a hillside. We were placed at wide intervals across a barren slope, be-cloaked with spears and shields in our hands, whilst the crew set up several hundred yards away for an extreme long shot. Ordered to stand rock still, the cold wound it's icy fingers into every bone and sinew. It seemed to take hours and I really did feel that I was beginning to succumb to hypothermia. Could it possibly get any worse? It could. A cloudburst of freezing rain.

Like startled ferrets, the crew scurried for cover in their snug trailers, then somebody remembered us.

'Don't move!' screamed the director, ' The positioning on this shot is critical. Cover them up.'

They found some large sheets of polythene which they spread over our heads, right to the ground, where the edges were weighted down with rocks. And there we stayed until the rain had passed. I remember thinking, as I stood there, the rivulets of sleet coursing down the polythene barely an inch from my nose, 'Is this any way for a grown man to make a living?'

Another production I shudder to recall found me in Saffron Walden one cold night. It was Britain under martial law and we were citizens under armed guard. There we were in the town square, locked in a big square cage with a metal mesh roof. Hoses were aimed into the air so that the water cascaded down onto our shivering bodies. I watched enthralled as icicles instantly formed from the drips that hung from the roof of our cage.

One of the most dreary productions I ever worked on, and many would agree with me I'm sure, involved repetitive days working on a set which had been constructed as a building site. The work was very boring and the scenes seemed to involve nothing more than the day to day life of a gang of labourers. As entertainment it seemed to us to be a recipe for disaster. Strangely enough, it turned out to be one of the funniest, best written television successes in years. It was called AUF WIEDERSEHN PET.

"ONLY FOOLS AND HORSES"
The Jolly Boys Outing to Margate

PRESTIGE

This should make a slim chapter. Prestige for a noddy is about as credible as Bernard Manning topping the bill at a Gay Rights convention.

My prestige on this side of the business has amounted to very little. In my appearances for the B.B.C. Shakespeare productions I bore a torch in HAMLET, carried a dead stag on a pole in TIMON OF ATHENS, and was a variety of cloaked figures in OEDIPUS, CYMBELINE and HENRY V1. I once had to hand Sir Laurence Olivier a sandwich but, alas, was pipped at the post for an Emmy. Along with others, I was directed by Harold Pinter for a filmed insert to be shown on stage during his SWEET BIRD OF YOUTH. Big deal.

I was asked if I could play the guitar for Elkie Brooks. This turned out to be me on a stool, guitar in hand, miming in silhouette whilst Elkie was superimposed over me. I didn't even get to meet her as her part was recorded later. In the pop quiz show NEVER MIND THE BUZZCOCKS, I was in a line-up of potential candidates for the contestants to decide which one of us was the real lead singer from the 70's pop band 'Kenny'. (Remember 'Do the Bump'?) Jonathan Ross and his team picked me. And I must mention my long running role in THE BILL. For years I was the regular milkman! Yes, whenever the boys in blue conducted a dawn raid or simply knocked at a door, you could guarantee that would be me driving by in the float (special skills for learning to do that) or looking surprised as I picked up the empties. Every now and then I would also appear in the same series as a passer-by, an irate neighbour, a fingerprint specialist, a doctor, a window cleaner, and a host of other guises. Holy smoke, that milkman was versatile!

A comedienne called Karen Kay (who flirted briefly with fame) was appearing in a live television variety show. Impersonating Frank Spencer, I had to walk on and hand her a bunch of flowers but was told to keep the blooms covering my face. Oh, musn't forget, I was a pair of gloved hands poking through a cardboard cut out for the LENA ZAVARONI SHOW. In THE DAY OF THE TRIFFIDS (B.B.C. version) I was one of the only people left on earth who could still see, but I still wasn't allowed to speak!

My appearance with Jeremy Irons was a biggy. A group of us were hired to dance the charleston for a garden party sequence set in the twenties. All morning we were taken through our paces by a choreographer and it seemed that we may have something of importance to do. After lunch, I alone was selected for a scene involving Jeremy Irons and his leading lady. However, this scene was to be played in close up so I was placed directly in front of them, with a light behind me, and was told to do the dance. Of course, I was not in shot. The idea was for me to cast flickering shadows across their faces. I felt a complete pillock but at least the crew found it amusing.

Mind you, I have had my share of lines to impart over the years. 'A cup of coffee, please', 'Look out!', 'Ahhhhhh!', 'Hang 'im!', etc., etc.. I have done plenty of training films with pages of dialogue but these are just for in-house purposes for various companies. Background agents often supply the cast for these epics (because we come cheaper than actors from bona fide agencies) but this means that one will often have heaps to do and a substantial role to play for not very much money. Also, one's performance never gets shown outside of the relevant factory or office. It might be something like 'Staff/ customer relations', 'How to sell' or 'Thirty uses for the multi-coil'. Still, it's nice to flex the ol' dramatic muscles once in a while.

When on location, the attitude of the general public can vary enormously. Actually, they are usually very accommodating when they encounter a film unit, especially if it is a well known programme and there are celebrities around. Sometimes I am amazed by the liberties that are taken by the assistants as they get people to co-operate with the filming. Holding up traffic for ages, stopping pedestrians from going about their business, preventing people from leaving or entering their homes, and so on. It seems that the whole world is expected to stop revolving so that the director can get his shot. Mind you, not everyone puts up with it with good grace. I remember some buskers who wouldn't move until they had been paid and other folk who refuse to wait an instant, exercising their 'rights' as they walk straight through takes.

The funniest incident I witnessed brightened up a dull shoot on THE BILL. (And I wasn't even playing the milkman that day!) We were filming a tree planting ceremony on some rough North London estate.

Suddenly, a young woman appeared with an ironing board which she set up right in the middle of the shot. She also had a pile of clothes with her which she commenced working on, using the iron, the flex and plug of which trailed away to nowhere. Deciding to ignore her, the director ordered the angle changed so that she would be out of view, but she was wise to this and moved accordingly. When this had happened twice more, the production manager went over to reason with her. This was like a red rag to a bull.

'Why should I bleeding move? I live on this estate and that's my flat over there, in shot without my permission. Who do you lot think you are? We've had you all over the years... THE SWEENEY, MINDER, ONLY FOOLS AND HORSES, and God knows how many times we've had your crap programme, coming down here patronising us with your posh cars and smoked salmon sandwiches. We've had enough of it.'

With the P.M. getting nowhere, the director thought he had best have a try. He made the mistake of offering her money.

'What? Trying to buy me off? What am I, a bloody whore?'

He tried a more subtle approach, telling her that THE BILL was a responsible and realistic programme which reflected the social problems of ordinary people.

'Oh yeh?' she laughed, pointing at two of the uniformed actors. 'Well, those two are nothing like real coppers. Their arses arn't fat enough!'

And so it went on. I'm not sure how it was resolved in the end but it got us an early lunch. (That story has reminded me to mention the method by which you can tell which policemen have been supplied by Central Casting. Yes, they are the ones wearing the outsized helmets and brown hush puppy shoes! Bit of an 'in' joke, that.)

One of the most tiresome situations is to be on location dressed in the uniform of a public servant. I dread anything on a railway station dressed as a porter because you can be sure that the populace will hone into you in their thousands to ask train times or with requests to carry their bags. Unlike some, I have never been wicked enough to send them onto wrong platforms or tell them where they can deposit their bags! I always meant to get a sign to hang around my neck... 'I am not real'.

CHECKING IN!
A common sight before the advent of mobile phones.

**NO MORE
QUEUEING!**

One sunny morning I was sitting outside a pub with a group of other 'customer' extras. It was one of those days when we hadn't been used so not a lot had happened. I felt a tap on my shoulder and there was an old man saying to me, 'I've been watching you lot for hours from my house over there. You havn't done a thing all day. Is this what I pay my T.V. licence for? It's a bloody disgrace!'

Sometimes, on the street, bright eyed folk will approach and ask how to become an extra. My answer nowadays is don't commit yourself until you have read this book!

We are often selected to play criminals in programmes like CRIMEWATCH, CRIME MONTHLY or TRUE CRIMES but this is done purely on physical resemblance to the said offender. I was shortlisted to play the Railway Rapist and was told that they would actually want to take blood from me in a medical sequence. It gave a whole new meaning to the phrase, 'What do they want... blood?' My brother was picked to be a child molester but decided against doing it when he thought of the likely reaction of other parents when he went to collect his own kids from school. It's a funny thing, but a lot of people seem to have great difficulty in seperating acting from reality.

I have been to many strange and interesting places countrywide but have never yet landed anything truly exotic and glamorous. The only television jobs I have had abroad were one in Denmark (and the town was closed on our free day) and one in Holland where I played a sea sickness victim on a ferry. I never get jobs like the group who were taken for weeks of filming in Tahiti for THE BOUNTY, or the man I know who had never been abroad in his life yet suddenly found himself whisked off to Switzerland, Spain, Mexico, Florida and Antigua for a three week photographic shoot. Your face just has to fit, that's all.

Actually, unless one is at the very top of the tree, there is not very much glamour and excitement in the film and television industry, but you can pick up handy skills. When I worked on NELSON, I, and about a hundred others, playing the Victory's gun crews, spent a week with an expert learning the exact procedure for operating 19th. century twelve pounder cannon. If Napoleon ever makes another comeback we'll be ready for him!

A word here on casting requirements. I once tried to phone a casting office direct to obtain some work on a production of BEAU GESTE which was being filmed in Dorset (!). I knew they needed legionaires and Toureag tribesmen, hordes of whom would be used during the attack on the fort. Being dark eyed, I thought with a bit of tanning, beard and robes I would fit the role. Stranger things have happened. However, I was informed, rather snootily, that the director had specifically asked for the real article, i.e. born and bred Arab Equity members who lived in the area. Obviously, Bournemouth must be over-flowing with bedouin thespians. In the end, I understand they recruited scores of middle eastern students from the local colleges. The final result on screen didn't so much look like savage, marauding tribesmen as end of term in the refectory.

JOBS AWAY

Now and again I have been engaged for jobs away from home but this began to happen less and less as the companies tended to use local people to save on expenses. Still, there have been occasions when nice ones have arisen, all found sojourns in hotels, etc., and I must say that, as a rule, they do look after you.

I remember a lovely two week job at the seaside for ONLY FOOLS AND HORSES which was like a paid holiday. The crew even did us the honour of going on strike for a few days , which gave us some extra dates and the chance to nip over to France on the razzle in the B.B.C.'s time.

My brother and I did a commercial together up in the Yorkshire Dales. We stayed in a beautiful little village, drank hot toddies and took in the scenery. It was really delightful except for the biting cold. In fact we were all shivering so much on film that we were re-engaged two months later to go back up there for a re-shoot. Then there was the Sun commercial in Devon. I had a few good friends on that one so it turned into a social whirl. We were also surrounded by page three girls. To cap it I even managed to get myself featured thus making a handsome profit in repeat fees.

I had a week in Cumbria on a promotional video for a new car. Good money, lovely hotel, one of Benny Hill's 'Angels' playing my wife... what more could you ask for? (Actually, this girl was Sue Upton, Benny's favourite.) So the game is not all doom and gloom. (Having said that, I remember spending a month in Tunbridge Wells one week-end, but that's another story!)

I also worked on THE CHRONICLES OF NARNIA which took in quite a few days all through one long, hot summer. We went to Snowdonia and to the Peak Cavern in Derbyshire and an interesting time was had by all. In spite of the fact that we spent much of the time underground filming in caves, I have done worse jobs. The director was a gentleman and showed consideration for our suffering in the ghastly costumes we had to wear. We were playing rock men and were dressed in tight, rubberized muscle suits, not unlike being entombed in a giant torniquet. The masks were rubber too, with slits for the eyes and tiny holes at the mouth through which to breathe. Instant claustrophobia,

"THE CHRONICLES OF NARNIA" (B.B.C.) Snowdonia 1990.

The wicked Queen's Rock Guards.
An example of the many different walks of life who are attracted to extra work.

From left to right:
The author, a promotions executive,
a marketing manager for Butlins
and a martial arts instructor.

Asleep deep in the bowels of the Peak Cavern,
Derbyshire. Well, it was about three in the morning!

but the money was good.

I was booked on MAGNUM once but my heart didn't flutter for long. Tom Selleck had come to London so the nearest I got to Hawaii was Maida Vale. I was booked on it again more recently but this time it turned out to be a commercial for the ice cream of the same name.

Speaking of awful costumes, I must mention the science fiction show BLAKE'S SEVEN on which I had about a week's work in a gravel pit somewhere near Reigate. This gravel pit was supposed to simulate Planet X or some such place, which says a lot for this particular show. We (five of us, I think) were playing freaks which had been created by a mad scientist. The costume involved a fitting for a death mask, an experience not to be recommended as it involves a plaster cast being made of the face, nose straws, the lot. Not very enjoyable. The face piece (hooked beak attached), was adhered to the flesh with a gooey substance previously unknown to me, a vast hairy attachment was then hung from the lips and chin and fangs were inserted. On top of this was placed a huge, bulbous helmet, also covered in hair, complete with curved horns which lit up. (Batteries were concealed in the helmet.) The main part of the costume involved a one piece, shaggy cat suit, paws and claws included, which we were sewn into, thus making visits to the toilet an impossibilty. Once you were in, you were in. Also, what with the face piece and fangs, eating was not exactly a breeze either. We had to resort to slurping liquids through straws.

By the end of each exhausting day, having spent our time pulling up trees, chasing each other about, sniffing and snarling, we were shattered and famished. One of the monsters was so effeminate he made Marilyn Monroe look butch. When he roared and raged, as we had been instructed to do, it sounded like a mewing kitten. After all this, all we wanted to do each evening was blow our expenses eating out lavishly. Within a day or two of getting home, I noticed a rash appearing on my face, particularly under my eyes where the bulk of the adhesive had lain. This got steadily worse until my features had glutinised into a mass of weeping sores. Pretty soon I discovered that my fellow monsters were suffering from the same affliction (in varying degrees) so it was obviously something to do with the make-up they had used so freely on us. Believe it or not, our agent advised us not to make waves, and, green as grass, we obliged. All except one chap who had the sense to take out a private action against the B.B.C. and won substantial recompense out of court. The rest of us didn't know about this until a long time afterwards but it was a powerful lesson.

This incident also brought with it an amusing by-product. Well, amusing now that I can look back on it. At the time, I was trying very hard to break into television comedy writing. I had experienced a near miss with a situation comedy series I had written and was beavering away trying to get sketches accepted for light entertainment shows. When my BLAKE'S SEVEN scabs were at their worst, I also had the misfortune to need some quite major dental surgery to remove an abcess, the result of which was that my mouth was full of stitches and my face was bruised and swollen up like a balloon. Regardless of this, I still managed to end up with a day's work at the B.B.C. but I kept my hideous features well in the background. Now, who should I bump into but my Uncle Bill who was a warm-up man. (That is, a comedian whose job it is to 'warm up' the audience in a studio before the main comedy show begins.) Although I could hardly speak, I managed to explain my predicament to my uncle and he was sympathetic. He suggested that we go to the B.B.C. club so that I could forget my pain in a cosy drink or two. At his invitation, we ended up in the V.I.P. bar and who should be there but the Head of Light Entertainment and the B.B.C.'s Chief Comedy Script Editor. Uncle Bill knew them both well and at any other time it would have been a golden opportunity for me to use a little family influence to peddle my wares; but looking like I did that day? Forget it. No amount of explanation seemed adequate. I felt it was very much a case of, 'Meet my nephew... Quasimodo!'

On the story of OPPENHEIMER, I did a couple of days filming in a top secret atomic research centre. The security was very tight and we were not even permitted to visit the toilet without a guard. As we entered an eerie underground bunker (echoes of QUATERMASS), a wild eyed, white coated boffin pinned little strips of paper to our lapels. When we asked about this he grinned like Dr. Death and said, 'Radiation warning. If it changes colour, you're in trouble.'

OTHER STRINGS TO THE BOW

There are times, when work is thin on the ground, when even the busiest noddy can be forced to take engagements outside of the business.

One alternative lies in promotion work. By way of a change, I was once called upon to appear in a department store as Cy-Kill, mortal enemy of the Gobots. The costume was beyond belief, almost seven feet high and made of solid wood. Every step was agony and the only means of vision was through a tiny slit of gauze. Inevitably, this meant that I blundered along through the toy section completely oblivious to the displays I was demolishing and the old ladies and children I was crushing underfoot. I was supposed to do a whole day of half hour on, half hour off, but the costume was so unbearable I ended up amending that to fifteen minutes on, forty five off.

In lean periods, signing on at the Unemployment Benefit Office is an option, but this is very complicated, what with declaring odd days of work, etc.. These days the authorities have made it so difficult for people in our profession that it is scarcely worth the aggravation of trying. (Even though we pay National Insurance like anyone else.) And so, when things get really tight, one might be forced to earn a few bob in whatever way one can. Odd jobs for cash are hard to come by but they can be found. One of the worst I had to do was three days unloading lorries which were filled to the roof with rolls of coloured industrial plastic sheeting. They weighed a ton and were really awkward to handle as the toxic dust filled up my lungs and eye sockets. A terrible, filthy, back breaking job which made me feel like I had been forced through a mangle and beaten with broken bottles. The money for this was a real pittance but it helped to put into perspective what a lot of poor souls have to put up with every working day of their lives. At least for me it was only very temporary. It made me loathe to complain the next time I was paid for sitting around doing nothing on a film set.

Some individuals I know do handy little jobs where they have an understanding with their employer, enabling them to take time off to noddy whenever the need arises. They are the lucky ones. Others are sent into a panic the minute the telephone stops ringing.

Once or twice, in desperation, I went after car delivery jobs but was surprised at how bad the money can be. I did once take a job as a chauffeur, ferrying a variety of V.I.P.s back and forth during the Farnborough Air Show. ('I won't be needing you tomorrow; I'm taking some clients to Sardinia for lunch.') Still, it was nice to have the use of a flash new car for a few days.

I spent the early hours of one morning inflating hundreds of balloons with helium for a London Transport promotion. At a given moment they were supposed to soar into the air but for some reason most of them decided to just drift wearily along the track.

Following a promising interview, I nearly took a temporary position one Christmas as a jewelery demonstrator in an Oxford Street store. It required the learning of a seven page script for the sales pitch, and the management emphasised that it was very important not to stray from one word of it. That was a shame. It was so bad, the opportunities to ad-lib were too wonderful to miss. The script was full of dreadful 'funnies' with instructions in brackets such as 'Pause here for laughs'.

Market research is another avenue but you need to be a certain type of person to stand all those hours on the phone irritating total strangers. Even worse are the countless selling jobs which are always available; insurance, advertising space, time share, etc.. I actually agreed to try it once (God, things must have been really bad!) for a company selling double glazing and conservatories. On my first evening there, I was shown to my position amongst a row of booths, each with a telephone and a heap of index cards which contained all the contacts I would be required to ring and persuade that 'our prod- uct' was just for them. Suddenly it came to me just how much I hated the intrusion of sales people bothering me at home. I find this kind of thing to be an insult to people's intelligence and I simply couldn't bring myself to do it. I left without having made a single call.

Fortunately, I have always had music to fall back on. I had worked in bands, duos or on my own for years, but at one point I had become so busy with extra work that I actually gave up gigging for a while, apart from one excursion back onto the boards when I played the bad cap- tain in the pantomime SINBAD THE SAILOR. A raging interest in a specialist style of country roots music revived my enthusiasm for play- ing and I took up my guitar again with gusto. What's more, I went back

(Photograph by Tim Goodings)

My country band
"PEACE ON THE PANHANDLE"

to the drawing board, spending many hours teaching myself bluegrass banjo and torturing the neighbours with my fiddle practice! I ran a pretty successful rootsy band for a couple of years and we gained a good reputation on the London circuit, playing at many events and supporting some big names of the day. From there I drifted back into the mainstream of clubs, theatres, hotels, military bases, holiday centres, theme parks, private parties, in fact anywhere they would have us! I worked mainly in two duos, one a kind of 60's/70's tribute and the other an offshoot of my specialized outfit but with a more commercial slant. The latter of these tended to get the more interesting engagements as we were called upon when something a little out of the ordinary was required.

My other passion for writing took up a great deal of my time. It took me five years to write an historical saga about the Vikings which proved to be too self indulgent for publication, but I enjoyed myself putting it together. I nearly cracked it with another novel, this time a total contrast about mercenaries in Honduras but in spite of my literary agent's praise, it didn't win over any of the big publishers. Once I even took on a female pseudonym to churn out a romance for Mills and Boon but even they didn't want my particular brand of slush. Short stories and articles poured out of my typewriter with varying degrees of success, along with numerous other writing projects, but getting into print has always been a hard game.

Also, I kept quite busy as a minstrel playing for King Henry Vlll banquets. These are mainly laid on by a professional touring company, Swansflight Productions, which is run by an amazing character who really does seem to think of himself as King Henry. The last of the great actor/managers! And the show itself is only a part of it. Travelling with a company that can vary from a cast of eight up to over twenty, we transform any venue into a Tudor banqueting room, complete with castle walls, banners, authentic crockery, wenches, battling knights, jesters, the lot. The hardest part is assembling and dismantling all of this, so it feels more like labouring than showbusiness. However, it has taken me to some interesting places and into some novel situations! We used to make regular visits to the continent, usually working the military bases in Germany and Holland. Once we spent nearly a month in Lanzarote and performed only one show, but that would make a story in itself! I'll leave that for the next book I've got in mind!

Much against my better judgement, I was sent to do one of these theme nights on my own. Having been told it would be a tasteful affair singing a few 'Hey nonny nos' to a family audience, imagine my shock when I discovered that it was a stag night for thirty blokes! I am sure you can picture how that went down with me in my tights!

CHARACTERS

Some of the characters in the business are somewhat larger than life. As I have said before, they come from all walks and have nick names to match. The Surrey Astronaut, the Hackney Lizard, the Leyton Buzzard, Doomwatch...these handles speak for themselves.

The Hoover is a gushing lady from the operatic chorus world whose appetite for food is superhuman. Apart from the wild, hungry eyes, she appears perfectly normal, yet when she is faced by the location caterers she becomes a force to be reckoned with. Table spreads of salad are devestated in seconds; eclairs, doughnuts, biscuits, you name it, are wolfed down as if a threat of famine is looming. With her, main courses always come in double helpings, slooshed down with two or three bowls of spotted dick and custard. She once showed us her wedding photographs and there she was, resplendent as the bride, with a sandwich in her hand!

Whilst on this subject, I must mention an individual who often wears a peaked, canvas cap. On one call, following afternoon refreshments, the extras were called back onto the set and he stood before the camera with his cap crooked and mis-shapen. Before he could stop her, a wardrobe assistant lifted the cap from his head to straighten it and several cream cakes tumbled out!

On a Central Casting call, at some high bred country estate, I remember two shady types discussing how best they could waylay a few pheasants from the grounds for sale in their local markets.

Joe (name changed to protect the guilty) was one of the first colourful characters I encountered in the noddy world. It was on a night call and I was talking to a couple of fellow extras on the coach while Joe, who had been employed to play a corpse, was stretched out asleep across the back seat. A young assistant (who must have been new to the job as he was particularly pleasant), approached us with news of what was happening on the set and when they might be getting around to our scene. He made the mistake of disturbing Joe's slumber.

'Wot der fok's goin' on?' grumbled Joe as he sat up blinking.

'Oh, Joe,' grinned the assistant amiably, 'I've just come to tell you that we'll be getting to your bit in about an hour.'

'An hour?! Wot toime is it now den? Wot?! Even moi woif don't speak to me at t'ree in der fokkin' mornin', y' shoit bag!'

'Er...sorry...I...'

'Oi'll give y' sorry. Where d'yer live?

The assistant looked worried. 'Why?'

'Cos o'im gonna come an' burn yer fokkin' house down, that's woi!'

Joe was not really the type to argue with. Middle aged, not tall, but built like a brick ablution, with the kind of face you could crack walnuts with. Strangely enough, he used to own a flower shop. I had these visions of him throwing old ladies out of the door with their floral displays, shouting, 'Stick 'em up yer arse, missus!'

He was on the Walk-On committee for a while and would do the rounds of the extras on calls, demanding to see their Equity cards. One showbizzy queen was outraged to be asked for his card by the likes of Joe and couldn't resist voicing a bit of sarcasm.

'Would you like to see my act as well?' he huffed but Joe's sparkling repartee soon silenced him.

'Don't get lippy with me, y' cont, or you'll be pickin' glass out of yer head.'

He began transferring his talents to working on unit security which, perhaps, was more in his line.

Then there was Dave, a youngish roughneck from the East End who had a voice like Arthur Mullard. Actually, he wasn't a bad bloke really and showed many signs of having a good heart, but you never felt you could trust or believe him. He was into fixing and selling everything from cars to fridges and he reckoned he had experienced just about all there was in life. I bought a car from him and having clinched the deal was told I wouldn't be getting the seats I had seen, or the steering wheel, or the actual wheels!

'Oh, an' you won't be getting that engine eever. Don't worry though. I've got a lovely engine I can stick in that. Ain't I good to you?'

Like a fool, I went along with it. Within two days it had let me down on a long journey, cost me a fortune in parts and had forced me to call out the R.A.C.. I had their recovery truck dump it outside his house.

'Seized engine?' he exclaimed. 'Bollocks! Sweet as a nut that engine. Leave it with me.'

The next day he phoned to say, ' 'ere, that engine's seized.'

'Yes Dave, I know.'

'Don't worry. You can pick up an engine for one of them dead cheap, whack it in an' you can still flog it for a profit.'

'Really? Tell you what...why don't you give me my money back, do what you said and **you** make the profit?'

He thought about this for a moment then said, 'If you weren't my mate, I'd tell you to piss off.' Which, of course, is what he was telling me anyway. But he did have one more bright idea.

'We can 'ave it squashed an' make it vanish. You can claim on the insurance.'

He waxed eloquent on many subjects, including Shakespeare.

'That Shakespeare bollocks? That ain't acting. It's all about cardboard trees an' stuff...'

I was with him and a girl singer and we were discussing fidelity in marriage.

'You wouldn't be unfaithful to your wife would you, Dave?' asked the girl. 'Don't you love her?'

'Course I do. I love steak an' kidney pie too, but I wouldn't want it every day for eight years.'

He actually vanished from the noddy scene some years ago when he was working on a programme in Scotland and had a very nasty accident. A camera crane tipped over and crushed him causing, by all accounts, permanent internal and back problems. He was fighting for compensation for years. I was told that Equity were handling the case for him but ceased representation when they made a startling discovery. Apparently, he was working under the guise of somebody else's identity and according to the birthdate they had on record, he was ninety two years old! I cannot swear to the truth of that as I have never seen him since. The last I heard, he was installing satellite television dishes. (And no doubt bringing mayhem to NATO's radar system!)

A mention here of Norman, a porky fellow who harboured serious acting ambitions. One day he said, 'I can't understand you people...content to be extras all your lives.'

'What would you do then, Norman,' asked someone, 'if you realised you weren't going to make it as an actor?'

Norman shook his head gloomily and made a slashing motion across each of his wrists. A comedian swiftly said, 'What, sub lieutenant in the navy?'

I must also include Danny, who used to advertise himself in the Stage directory as 'The Master of Mimicry', claiming he could impersonate anyone from Mr. Spock to Prince Charles. By his own admission, he was once contacted by a man who wanted a celebrity look-alike to open his new store. He asked for an Arthur Daley and, needless to say, Danny said he, personally, could fit the bill. The man also asked for his Arthur Daley to arrive driving a Jag and Danny said this could be arranged. On the big day, the crowds were waiting outside the store, a huge banner proclaiming Arthur Daley's presence, when along comes Danny, in his trilby and sheepskin coat, waving out of the window of his little green citroen!

'Sorry,' he mumbled, 'couldn't get the jag.'

The store owner was dumbfounded. 'Arthur Daley?!' he roared. 'You're nothing like him! I've been done!'

He has also been known to bring his own canvas director's chair onto sets, complete with his name on the back. On another occasion he was booked by a big time photographer for his Christopher Lee interpretation only to find himself dressed as Dracula, acting the stooge and collecting the coats of guests at the man's private party.

Danny was responsible for subjecting me to one of the most embarrassing moments of my life. Three of us (including he) were booked on THE MANAGERESS, the television series about the female boss of a football team. Myself and the other extra, who I know well, were doing our best to avoid him but it wasn't easy, there being so few of us. Danny kept hanging around irritating us with unwanted tales about the agency he was setting up. As we talked, with Danny fidgeting beside us, who should walk by but that fine actress and star of the show, Cherie Lunghi. Danny waited until she was a good ten feet past us then he shouted, 'Oi, Cherie!'

She stopped and turned to face us, her expression one of bewilderment. 'Sorry?' she mused pleasantly. 'Did you call me?'

Danny nodded and crooked his finger in a beckoning gesture. Incredibly, she actually responded and came over to join us. My friend and I were already cringeing in dreaded anticipation.

'ere, Cherie,' he said, charmlessly, 'do you ever do any theatre?'

This to an actress who has probably trod more boards than a whole season of tourists on Brighton pier.

'Well,' replied Ms. Lunghi, with what must have been a vast dollop of tolerance, 'it has been known.'

Danny leaned in close to give a loud stage whisper in her ear. 'Good. Listen,' he leered, narrowing his eyes earnestly, 'my parents have just opened a nice little theatre on the south coast and they're gonna be looking for actresses. So...' he gave an oily grin and a wink, 'you might be hearing from your agent.'

We nearly vanished through a crack in the floor. Luckily, being a civil person, she went through the charade of thanking him before going on her way. As my friend and I gazed at him in horror, Danny smirked and said to us, 'You've got to keep in with these people.'

It can be well imagined what hilarity that story must have brought when she told it over lunch to the V.I.P.s.. Those bloody extras! This is exactly what I mean when I speak of how we all get tarred with the same brush.

His Dracula story reminds me of what happened to my good mate Phil when he reluctantly accepted a job as Superman, handing out leaflets for a publicity stunt. What he didn't know was that he was expected to spend the whole day traipsing around the West End, on foot, barging into the offices of a mammoth list of film and advertising companies, in character. The stick he received from the passing population was horrendous as he slopped around in the rain, his tights and cloak

EXTRA TYPES

all baggy. He was even stopped by Japanese tourists to pose for photographs. Worst of all, he bumped into two girls who he hadn't seen since the days when he was a successful recording artiste. They had laboured under the misapprehension that he had gone on to better things. Squirming with embarrassment, he had to tell them that he had just finished filming a commercial in which he was featured and had lost the unit.

Actually, Phil's career as an extra was a very temporary phase and it's not really fair to speak of his recording career in the past tense. He did put that side of his life on ice for a while but he certainly resumed it again and now has his own recording and publishing company. In fact he is one of the most positive and enterprising people I know and was never destined to spend long in a loser's business. Even so, he was quite a character on the noddy scene until he moved to America then back to his native North East of England where he returned to singing professionally. He once had his own hairdressing business and drove a Rolls Royce for a while. It was great watching the reaction of assistants when he turned up on calls in it. An extra with a Roller. Wonderful! Moving back down South he gradually built a name for himself in the world of Personal Development and became a top selling author on the subject. He has published six highly successful books, is in great demand for his motivational lectures and seems to go from strength to strength. Naturally, he is a target for criticism from certain bitter and cynical noddies who will be walking past the cafe window in EASTENDERS for the rest of their lives, but I feel total admiration for him.

Jimmy was a children's entertainer, standing about five feet tall with a sinister smile and penetrating eyes that possessed a hint of madness. His manner was very overbearing and I am amazed that he never got thumped by anybody. I had first worked with him years before at Butlin's and thought him a pain in the backside then, but when he reappeared as a fellow stand-in on TOP OF THE POPS I could scarcely credit his behaviour. During rehearsals, the band Status Quo were tuning up on stage when Jimmy marched up to them and collared their lead singer, Francis Rossi, in the manner of a policeman.

'Hello. I'm Jimmy. Who are you?'

Rossi, totally flummoxed, greeted him politely but was answered with,

'Pop group, eh? Famous? Well, I've never heard of you.'

On the same show we had Adam and the Ants during their brief flirtation with fame. Adam must have thought Armageddon had arrived when he was confronted by Jimmy. He insisted on introducing me.

'Here you are, Adam. My friend Mike plays the guitar. I'm sure you two will have bags to talk about.' Then he promptly stalked away and left us to it. An awkward moment to say the least.

I was once stuck with him on a private airfield for a photographic job which would have been a dream, had it not been for his presence. We were doing the brochure for a new executive jet and he and I had to portray the businessmen getting wined and dined on board. Although we never actually got off the ground, it was a very nice job. We were treated well and the surroundings were luxurious, but Jimmy had to stick his oar in. At one point we were sitting in the V.I.P. lounge, all very posh, when a small jet landed and the party on board disembarked. The central figure was a tall, silver haired chap who oozed sophistication and an air of authority. He was obviously a man of considerable importance; could have owned the airline for all I know.

'I say,' bellowed Jimmy, noting the fur hat this V.I.P. was wearing, 'are you a Russian?'

The man was taken aback but Jimmy had no intention of easing his assault. Pointing at the fat cigar the V.I.P. was holding he said, 'There's no smoking in here, you know.'

'I don't see any signs,' came the reply in a voice that was obviously accustomed to giving orders not receiving them.

'Maybe not, but there's three of us sitting here and we arrived first. None of us smoke so you're outvoted. Now, if you don't mind, either put that cigar out or leave.'

I caught my breath, but incredibly the man did as he was told and left the building. It just shows what you can achieve if you show enough front. Jimmy, of course, was totally convinced that he had done the right thing. 'Smoking! Filthy habit! Somebody should tell him that it's bad for his health.'

A bit later, one of the photographer's assistants came over to pass a few minutes with us. I am sure he must have regretted it. He told us a joke, the tag of which included a well known four letter expletive. Jimmy was not amused.

'Did you say the "C" word?'

The assistant looked quizzical. 'What? You mean "C..."?'

Jimmy gasped with shock. 'You said it again! Didn't your parents bring you up to realise that swearing is a sin?'

You see, Jimmy was also a born again Christian of the worst kind who delighted in preaching to the world. He loved an argument so there was no point in trying to stave him off with normal conversation. When he got married I received a full report from another children's entertainer who had been invited to the reception. Apparently, it was an afternoon affair where they served Tizer and played party games.

Another regular on the scene was Roy, a very fit entertainer in his sixties, who worked a speciality cowboy style act using whips and such. He had an amazing past, the kind of life that could make you feel insignificant. (As if extra work isn't enough to do that to you!) In the 1930s he had been a cavalryman in India fighting hill tribesmen. At the outbreak of World War 2 he was sent with the first British Expeditionary Force into France and narrowly escaped death at Dunkirk. He then became a physical training instructor (incidentally, he was a keen sportsman who was still running half marathons, and had competed in the 1936 Munich Olympics where he actually met Hitler!), volunteering for sabotage work and emerging as a pioneer member of the legendary Special Air Service regiment. As a trooper in this elite force, he partook in many raids on enemy installations and spent weeks behind enemy lines posing as a French civilian during the preparations for "D" Day. When the S.A.S. was reformed during the Korean War, he was called back in as an N.C.O. and was captured and tortured by the Communists. He gave a very detailed description of this which made my hair curl!

Having led such a colourful life, it seemed strange to me that he could tolerate being pushed around by snot nosed assistants, but he took it all in his stride. He also supplied wartime military vehicles to film and television companies. One morning, at about 6.00am., he was sitting in one of his jeeps waiting for the unit to arrive, when he spotted a teenaged yob breaking into a car. When Roy strolled over to investigate, the yob made the mistake of taking a swing at him. Naturally, it was nothing to a man of Roy's expertise to turn this delinquent upside down and hold him helpless with a foot to the throat. A passerby fetched the police but when they arrived, they seemed more concerned about the slight bruising on the yob's neck than they were with Roy's public spirited action. Unbelievably, he was charged with assault! Roy was very disillusioned by this. No wonder people are so reluctant to go to one another's aid.

Ralph the Mouth was a strange one. He would often bring a guitar on calls and drive us all crackers in the dressing room with his songs. He never seemed to be quite of this planet, but I can't forget one classic statement he made; 'I'm not gay, but honestly, I have to confess, if it meant getting on...to get a major part, say, and the director fancied me...well, I would take it up the arse...just a bit.'

Veronica, by contrast, is a very interesting lady who would come and go into the noddy world inbetween her many and varied trips abroad. She would take off alone doing such things as roughing it in India, working as a teacher in Greece and writing a book in Spain. She has had at least one of her plays performed on Radio 4 and once worked as a private detective. Completely changing direction, she studied and qualified as a homoeopath and set up her own private practice. I think she uses her life to the full but she is very modest and won't agree with me.

And then there is Hugo, a sad scrawny individual who wallows in delusions of grandeur. When not showing off his 'water on the knee', he might be regaling us with his Frank Sinatra impression or passing around the proofs of his latest photo session. These contact sheets are an education. Dozens of shots of him in a huge array of outfits; costermonger, German storm-trooper, gangster, Japanese admiral, commando, but all of them looking exactly like Hugo with different hats on.

His performance in the B.B.C.'s HAMLET should be etched in television history. It was a massive scene involving scores of extras and virtually the entire prestigious cast. Derek Jacobi, as the noble Danish prince, had launched into one of the Bard's impressive, rambling monologues. The cameras were rolling, sweat formed on Jacobi's brow as he gave it his all, the minutes ticked by... it was a powerful and demanding performance. Then, the taut atmosphere was shattered by a roar from the floor manager. 'Hold it! Who's that idiot behind the Queen?!'

It was Hugo, framed clearly over Claire Bloom's shoulder, in full courtier's costume, still wearing his large, horn rimmed glasses!

A lot of ex-dancers and actresses who married rich men still do the work either for pin money or out of sheer boredom. There also tends to be a liberal sprinkling of comedians, usually ones who are struggling to make a living in the clubs. Get stuck in a dressing room with a bunch of them trying to outdo each other with gags and it is quite a brain numbing experience.

Musn't forget poor old Billy. He was never anything much in show-business, though he loves to tell everyone about all the names he has worked with in the past. His behaviour on sets makes the skin crawl and he still seems convinced that he is going to make it some day. This he attempts to achieve by making sure that he is seen in every shot. He always worms his way to the front, peering over shoulders and around corners, emphasising his appearance with the most terrible over the top expressions. He wears outlandish clothes (loud checked suits which would make a bookmaker look conservative) and props like monocles and ridiculous huge pipes to get himself noticed. Pathetic really. Then there is his embarrassing collection of photograph albums, full of shots of him with his arm awkwardly around dozens of irritated or bored looking celebrities. He appeared on a television documentary once talking about his life as an extra and showing these bloody albums! That must have done our image the world of good.

I know of one man who, in his desperation to earn as much as possible, seriously considered donning a curly wig and glasses so that he could work as two people!

But, of all the facets of humanity to be found amongst the extra's ranks, there is one particular type who always stood out, to me, as the most tiresome and distasteful. They were best described as the Central Casting 'barrow boy' fraternity. By this I don't mean to decry all those who man a barrow for a living, but the expression is somehow explanatory. Approaching (or past) middle age, probably from East or 'Sarf'

London, they wear 'shades', have beer bellies and a way of standing around, coat collars up, eyes darting everywhere, lips drawn studiously back over teeth as they make snide comments about everyone else. They have their own language which appears to have been lifted from a below par episode of MINDER. 'Know wot I mean?', 'It's a blinder', 'My ol' woman...', 'Wot's the score?', 'Gotta be wurf a century, ennit?', 'Fuck orf!', etc., etc.. If not 'duckin' an' divin' ', they are to be found embroiled in endless card games which they resent leaving when called on to the set. They are the ones who avoid everything they can, look and act the worse in costume, push in the queues and yet have the biggest mouths and give out the most abuse when it comes to demanding payment. They hate 'poofs' and 'spades', love to preach their streetwise code, yet think nothing of circulating 'ooky gear', laughing at the so called 'wallies' they've turned over. They favour fake designer watches and will always have a few to sell. Oh yes, these boys know all the angles and are oh, so macho!

Many of them are Equity members, and yet it's obvious that they could never have possibly done anything in the business. They have bent cards, obtained by many means. Anyone new to the game is resented out of hand and considered a 'wally', because the most infuriating thing about this bunch is that they are convinced that the whole noddy business belongs to them alone and anyone else is muscling in on their territory. It seems they like to think of themselves as a sort of cross between Arthur Daley, Del Trotter and Reggie Kray, only they lack the required humour and strength of character. 'Jack the Lads' who would perish if the word 'fuck' was removed from the English language.

I am told there is room for everybody, but I just wish there was no room for them.

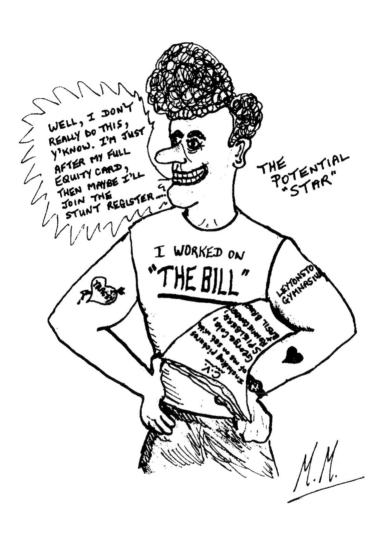

CELEBRITIES

I guess the time has come to indulge in a spot of name dropping. Well, perhaps name dropping is hardly the operative phrase as I could not consider myself a bosom buddy of the well known faces I have encountered as a noddy. However, by the law of averages, I have worked in close proximity to many 'stars' too numerous to name in full, as would anyone in the game. In any case, there would be no reason to compile such a list. Instead I will limit myself to a basic rundown of incidents worth a mention. I'm not in the business of muck-raking, otherwise I would probably be making a career out of writing for the tabloids, so please don't be disappointed if I don't stir up too much dirt. There **are** limits. Mr. Nice Guy, that's me!

Having said that, I can't resist including a few examples of unnecessary nastiness. Like anyone, I can only speak as I find. For instance, did Leonard Rossiter really need to say, when asked at an Equity meeting to hear out a member of the Walk-On committee, 'I thought this was a professional union. We are talking about the dog, not the flea on the end of it's tail'. Hmmm...that didn't gain him any new fans in the noddy ranks.

Coming from a showbusiness family, I was never impressed by the mere presence of celebrities, but when you have been doing background work for a while, you get so used to the constant barrage of familiar people it doesn't mean a thing. It's all in a day's work. To set the scene, I had best fill in a few more details about my past.

My father was a successful variety performer in the 1950s who also did a great deal of work on radio and television. He was known as George Martin, the Casual Comedian, and though I do say so myself, I can honestly state that his act was first class and original, his success based on an ability to come up with an endless supply of topical material. With his pipe and newspaper, seated at a piano or playing his accordian, he became a very familiar face. He was great in pantomime and he wrote some good songs too. His career really should have carried on to much greater heights than it did, but alas, he was a fool to himself, and for various reasons his name faded from the public eye whilst his contemporaries, who for years had been lower down the bill than him, carried on to fame, fortune and longevity. In the 60s, he found a new niche for his talents as a scriptwriter and for a long time he was much in demand writing shows and material for the likes of Jimmy Tarbuck, Harry Worth, Dave Allen, Rolf Harris, Tommy Cooper and many more. I have a tape of his radio show, SOUVENIR, on which he interviews George Raft, having written this legendary, gangster film star's stage spot at the Palladium.

One of his main achievments took the shape of being the sole writer of the BASIL BRUSH SHOW, a position he held from the very beginning through thirteen years of this foxy marionette's staggering success. The man behind (or below!) Basil, one Ivan Owen, was a lovely chap who sounded just like his right arm in real life. He and Dad were close friends for years, until suddenly, and very mysteriously, Ivan seemed to undergo a radical personality change. To Dad's bewilderment, Ivan turned against him, and in spite of the show's continuing success, brought in new writers. Eventually, Dad was given the total heave-ho which left him puzzled, somewhat poorer and not a little bitter, considering all the effort he had put into helping to create the character. He had stayed faithful to the show all along and had turned down several nice work opportunities so as to honour his committment to Ivan. In return he just had the door slammed in his face. It was interesting, and gratifying, to note that very soon after Dad's ousting, the BASIL BRUSH SHOW's popularity wained dramatically and disappeared from the screen.

As a child, I was used to show people. I have many memories of dressing rooms, sitting in the corner at showbiz parties, band calls and leggy dancers. My brother and sister recall when they were taken black berrying by Michael Bentine. Having picked the bushes clean, they were faced with the problem of where to store all the berries, but Bentine solved this by visiting a nearby shop to buy about twenty quarter pound bags of assorted sweets. The sweets were dumped onto the back seat of his car and the bags were used to hold the berries.

There are recollections of shows with the Goons when Spike Milligan brought a horse on stage during Dad's act. David Nixon became a very close friend of Dad's, probably his best in the business. He wrote David's magic shows for many years and they even toured the Far East together. I remember David as a quiet, easy mannered gentleman. Dad was devestated when he died.

My Dad ... GEORGE MARTIN
(The Casual Comedian)

In 1986, whilst writing for ventriloquist Keith Harris, Dad suffered a massive stroke which left him paralysed down his right side and unable to speak. It was a cruel blow to a man whose life revolved around words, humour and socialising and it was a very long time before I was able to come to terms with it. Ironically, seated in his wheelchair, he looked a picture of health, better than he had looked for ages. He certainly knew what was going on. His reactions were fine and he became very popular with the staff and other patients at the Royal Star and Garter Home in Richmond, Surrey, where, as an ex-serviceman, he became a resident. I am pleased to say that he lost none of his old charm (nor his taste for Bell's whiskey!) but I would have given a lot to be able to have a conversation with him again. Life, as they say, can be a bitch.

When he was stricken, one of the first people who rushed to visit him was Benny Hill. This surprised me as Dad had not had a lot to do with Benny in recent years, but the gesture was much appreciated and sent Mr. Hill up in my estimation several notches. He received many well known visitors in the early days of his illness, but as time went by, it soon became clear who his true friends were. A faithful few came regularly, but there were others, who were regarded as close, who, as far as I know, never showed their faces. Some said they wouldn't be able to cope with seeing him in such a condition, but that struck me as a pretty selfish viewpoint. The biggest accolade must go to the Beverley Sisters, bless 'em, who visited him religiously almost every week (unless they were working) and were a great tonic. I know they can conjure up an image of Donald Duck's nephews in full flight (and I say this with the greatest affection!) but they were wonderful and my gratitude to them knows no bounds.

In 1991, Dad contracted lung cancer and died. As a prominent member of the Grand Order of Water Rats, this showbusiness charity brotherhood gave him a wonderful send off and his funeral resembled a Who's Who of showbusiness. The following year they even put on a memorial show in his honour at the Churchill Theatre, Bromley, which was a sell out, the proceeds of which went to the Star and Garter. Some lovely things were said and it was a very moving experience. However, my brother and I, having been promised tickets, were shocked to find that, on our arrival, our seats had been given away! We never got to the bottom of that one, but in desperation, with the overture already playing, the sympathetic Front of House manager ushered us into the lighting box to watch the show over the shoulder of a hairy technician. Incredible. Extras to the end!

I have already mentioned the attitude of many performers regarding extras but I would like to add that the situation is not always as cut and dried as one might think. A lot of actors and actresses are decried because they do not talk to the extras, but this is stupid. Why should they? As long as the principals are not outwardly pig ignorant I'm not bothered if they don't make a bee-line for me. Anyway, much of the time the cast have enough to think about, the pressure of the part they are playing for instance, without having to pay lip service to the delicate sensitivities of a noddy's ego. Some 'stars' are accused of being miserable but I am not convinced that this is always fair, especially if this opinion is based on only one days experience of the person. We all have our off periods, after all, and these 'stars' are only human. A moments pre-occupation can be enough to send a noddy away with horror stories about a particular celebrity. 'Him? Right nasty so and so...' when all that individual might have done was to be concentrating on their job. The trouble is, when you are in the public eye, you are on trial all the time. There will forever be somebody who wants to drag you down. It's the price of fame.

Usually, the bigger the name, the nicer they tend to be. It is more often the intermediate, smaller part characters who create problems, but I look upon that as their own hang-up. I guess the big stars have nothing to prove and have left all their bitterness and sniping behind. Having said that, there is one very famous actress who revels in the publicity of her own image. Extras are instructed not to even look in her direction or address her in any shape or form. This is sickening.

A similar situation arose when Madonna and Sean Penn were in England filming SHANGHAI SURPRISE. Their obsession with privacy bordered upon paranoia and the media did all they could to fan the flames and worsen the problem. Everyone on the set was searched for cameras and a female reporter, who was found hiding in the toilet at one location with a tape recorder, was roughed up and ejected onto the street. Amidst all the hype and mayhem, as the charming twosome ran the gauntlet to avoid attention (it makes you wonder why they are in

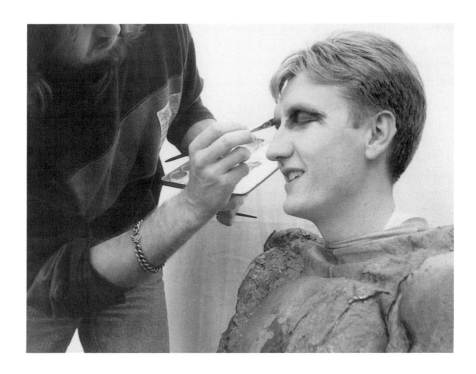

An extra having his eyes sealed shut for daring to look at the star of the show!

the business in the first place if they find it so traumatic to be gawked at), it was interesting to observe a lone figure sitting virtually unnoticed in the corner. George Harrison, as producer of the film, took it all in, no doubt very philosophically. Whatever happened to Beatlemania? (To balance this, it's only fair to state that Madonna appeared to have mellowed by the time she was making EVITA.)

As I said before, most of the bigger stars do tend to be approachable, providing their minders allow it. I am actually not at all interested in passing the time of day with celebrities just for the sake of it as I find it embarrassing and meaningless. Most full time noddies would agree with me here, but there are still enough naffs in the game who plague them for autographs and bore them with inane chat to add fuel to our already bad reputation.

The worst example of this I can think of occured on a picture called A MIRROR CRACKED, a large call with a crowd of F.A.A. extras playing guests at a posh garden party. Elizabeth Taylor arrived on set and received the rare honour of a round of applause as she took her place. Unfortunately, she found herself momentarily collared by a complete pillock. He wasn't even an extra but was the visiting boyfriend of one. The hapless Miss Taylor beamed as he approached her, but before her entourage could hustle him away, he was able to blurt out, 'So you're Elizabeth Taylor, eh? I thought you were supposed to be beautiful. You look like nothing more than a fat old bag to me.'

Not that I make a habit of playing big scenes with the stars, of course, but often, during a day's shoot, one can find oneself positioned close enough to an individual where opportunity and basic human courtesy allows for the passing of a few words. This happened to me on a television mini series called ELLIS ISLAND when I spent quite a while in the company of Richard Burton. In spite of the fact that he was obviously very ill, he proved to be most charming and friendly. Alas, this was to be his last appearance as he was dead within a few weeks.

The scene involved an entrance into a ballroom, and Richard Burton was to come through the door with Faye Dunaway on his arm. I, along with an extra named Sally, were to enter with them. Following a couple of rehearsals, an assistant took us to one side and told Sally she was being replaced in that particular shot by another girl. When Sally, just out of curiousity, asked why, the assistant said, 'Well, frankly, it's because you're better looking than Miss Dunaway. It takes the edge off her entrance.'

Another massive star who often endears himself to the crowd is Sean Connery. Unlike many big names, he has an incredible presence, an aura of stardom, yet he is also somehow very down to earth and genuinely likeable. When I worked on his picture THE RUSSIA HOUSE, I was amused by the contrast between him and his co-star, Michelle Pfeiffer, who was virtually unknown at that time. It was a hard day and the location was very oppressive. Mr. Connery took it all in his stride but Miss Pfeiffer seemed to be having problems and made sure everyone knew about it, serving as a classic comparison of the old school with the new school. (Mind you, being as it's the lovely Michelle, I'll make allowances!)

I played one of Hitler's personal bodyguards on the sequel to THE DIRTY DOZEN, called, predictably enough, THE DIRTY DOZEN'S NEXT MISSION. Lee Marvin was once again cast in his role as Reisman, but as the two films were made nearly twenty years apart, the difference showed. In the original, Marvin turned in an excellent performance as the tough officer but this time around it was sad to behold. By now, he was an old, visibly sick man who had to sit down between takes. Apparently, he was suffering from a chronic back problem. Even so, it must be said that he was friendly, full of character and had time for everybody.

The same thing could be said of James Cagney who was brought out of retirement to play a police chief in RAGTIME. He was so decrepit that he needed a double for any scenes which required him to walk more than a few paces.

Other names, who from personal experience deserve mention as being particularly likeable, include Michael Caine, Sir John Mills, Jim Henson, Roy Kinnear, Michael York, Lulu and Gordon Jackson who I worked with on THE PROFESSIONALS. I was one of only two extras employed that day and, as such, was expecting to be ignored as usual. However, Gordon Jackson actually made a point of chatting with me and seemed genuinely interested in what I had to say. I ended up quite matey with him. Norman Wisdom had a similar attitude when he was playing a straight part in a television play called GOING GENTLY. He actually came over to the extra's table and asked if he could join us for lunch. When I stood in as a panelist on WHAT'S MY LINE?, I spent a morning sitting alongside Lord Lichfield and we chewed the fat for a while. He seemed like an all round 'good egg'. Must pop round to see his cousin Liz sometime!

And as for Dame Barbara Cartland, well! She turned up on the set of the filming of one of her novels with the producer, Lord Grade, in an enormous limousine. Dressed all in pink and resembling an embalmed candy floss, she insisted on introducing herself to all of the extras. It was a big crowd too but that didn't seem to phase her. To be honest, for all her eccentricity, she was charming. Oliver Reed was there as well, with his new young wife, impeccably behaved and 'on the wagon' so I was unable to witness any of his legendary yobbishness.

The late Marti Caine proved to be a nice lady. I was the only Walk-On on an episode of her short lived series HILARY and she took the trouble of inviting me to lunch with her party. I didn't wish to impose on the rest of her companions, for regardless of her doubtless kind intentions, I felt sure that the others might not really wish to dine with a noddy. With no desire to be resented, I politely declined.

This reminds me of a dilemma which confronted me when I appeared in a pair of light entertainment shows called ARRIVALS. Thanks to my Dad, who was the script associate, I succumbed to a rare bout of nepotism and landed a speaking part. (The only other role he ever got for me was as a cockney coster monger on THE KEITH HARRIS SHOW.) The shows had a weird format. Set in an airport departure lounge, a group of celebrities (i.e. Hope and Keen, Ronnie Dukes, Carol Lee Scott, Norman Collier, other cabaret types of the era and me!) indulged in banter and sketches inbetween spots by variety artistes new to television. It was an interesting idea which could have led to a series but it didn't really work, the critics panned it and that was the end of that. During rehearsals I witnessed an example of the other side's attitude towards background artistes. The producer/director had this to say just as we were about to do our first run through...

'In the background you'll have to contend with about twenty extras. Them you can just kick!'

This brought laughs from all present save me. I lowered my head and bit my lip. The director was unaware that I did extra work but the

THE BRITISH BROADCASTING CORPORATION
BROADCASTING HOUSE, LONDON, W.1

TELEGRAMS: BROADCASTS LONDON TELEX ★ CABLES: BROADCASTS LONDON-W1 ★ TELEX: 22182
TELEPHONE: LANGHAM 4468

Michael Martin Esq.,   17th.October,1966

"Bricklayers Arms",

Ash, Near Aldershot,

Hants.

                    "SOUVENIR" BBC LIGHT PROGRAMME
                    TRANS.TUES. 18th.Oct.1966.

Dear Michael Martin,

Thankyou for your contribution to our programme "SOUVENIR".

I enclose a non-contract facility fee of £1.1s (One Guinea),

and regret that the last minute arrangements precluded the

inclusion of your name in the programme.

We enjoyed your singing and playing and hope you will continue

to persevere with your efforts in the musical field.

                         Yours faithfully,

                         J. Holles. (Producer)
                              (R,P.Prods.)

J.H./ M.Pk.

MY VERY FIRST PROFESSIONAL FEE!
I sang "Five Foot Two, Eyes of Blue" and played the ukelele
on my Dad's Radio Show. (Dad whistled the solo!) I was
twelve years old. Note that even then, as a performer,
my name was not in the credits!

116

message was perfectly clear. When the shows were being recorded, I naturally knew the extras who had been engaged to mill around as airport passengers. Two weeks before and it could easily have been me amidst their ranks and when ARRIVALS was over it would be me again. This is where my predicament arose. Who was I to spend breaktimes and lunches with? By now I was used to taking my meals with the other principal artistes and knew them well, but if I was seen doing this, the attitude of the other noddies would be, 'Who does he think he is?' On the other hand, if I sat with the extras, those very same souls would think I was being patronising. Catch 22. How could I win? I ended up drifting between the two groups like an aimless nomad.

During the course of my daily drives out to Elstree for this extravaganza, my clapped out Escort finally gave up the ghost. Carol Lee Scott, the outsized comedienne, solved this problem by giving me a lift in her car for the rest of the run. Carol became a friend, as did her husband, and I am pleased that she went on to do well in children's television as Grotbags the Witch.

Bob Monkhouse has, I think, been greatly misjudged in the past. He has suffered from a television reputation of smarminess and insincerity which does him no credit at all. In fact, his stage act is extremely slick, surprisingly blue, yet full of clever, topical satire. As a technical comedian I don't think he can be bettered. I first met him when I was a Butlin's redcoat in the early seventies, and he spoke to me about my father who he said he had always admired. The next time I saw him was years later when I was standing in as a dummy contestant on the pilot show of FAMILY FORTUNES. He remembered everything about our first meeting and we had a nice chat about showbusiness. His brain is incredibly receptive. I'm really pleased that he seems to have been rediscovered, and following some well received television appearances has earned the respect of the younger comedy fraternity. It's okay to like him now.

Jim Davidson, by contrast, is from a completely different mould. He seems to delight in vulgarity. I don't deny he has talent, chirpiness and the ability to tell a story but to me his act is pure schoolboy smut. Lots of old gags beefed up with foul language. Of course, he is immensely popular and brings the house down wherever he appears, so who am I to critiscise? I suppose that's why THE SUN is the highest selling newspaper in Britain, God help us! Dislike of this kind of tat has nothing to do with being prudish.

When my dad's second wife was introduced to him he greeted her with, 'I s'pose a fuck's out of the question?' I once saw him brought on stage during the warm-up for his television show. The audience was full of old dears and coach parties but that didn't stop the delightful Davidson from walking up to a woman in the front row, taking her hand and saying, 'Sorry if my fingers are wet, love. I've just had a piss.'

I worked on THE GENERATION GAME with him and heard that the agent was warning females about his offensive behaviour. He **is** friendly and approchable but during rehearsals he 'plays to the gallery' and the crew, naturally, love his constant swearing and obscenities, regardless of who else might be within earshot. I've actually been on his various shows several times and once had to share a bed with him. What an accolade! Still, it got me a Walk-On 2!

I spent a pleasant couple of days with Morecambe and Wise. Eric, particularly, was an old pal of Dad's so that was an 'in' for me. He was very aware of his health at the time and so he gave me and my fellow Walk-On the wine that had been provided for him. I remember Ernie talking a lot about money which made me think they were not that much different from their television personas.

Other impressions I have had of people on this side of the business include Bruce Forsyth's dislike of being upstaged, Larry Grayson's nervous energy (I was knocked black and blue as he manhandled me during THE GENERATION GAME!), Dick Emery's barely concealed 'eye for the birds' and Tommy Cooper's drinking. Mind you, boozed or not, Tommy's comic genius was never diminished. And then there's Frank Carson who is a pure gag machine. His whole life seems to revolve around their telling, even whilst queueing for a cup of coffee.

I once had the dubious distinction of being severely reprimanded by Eric Sykes. He was directing as well as starring in one of his T.V. specials and I was involved in a sequence where myself and an actor, as railway porters, had to lift a coffin from a train. This scene was covered from all angles and eventually the unit moved on to something else. Nobody said anything to me so I assumed that we had finished. Ambling away to find the tea urn, I heard my name being called over

'ARRIVALS" (A.T.V.)

My brief flirtation with
national television fame,
soon to become
"Departures"!
Next to me is singer Patsy
Ann Scott who was later to
become Mrs. Eddie Large
(of Little and Large),
Carole Asti and Reg Lloyd,
who had toured Germany
with my Dad in the 1949
show "Buttons and Bows".

With Carol Lee-Scott ("Grotbags")

the bull-horn. Dashing back, I had to scramble over the railway tracks to where a very irate Eric Sykes was waiting. He began to berate me in front of the crew, lecturing me on being unprofessional, the whole bit. I tried to explain, but the problem was that Eric was as deaf as a post and he either had his hearing aid out or switched off. Everything I said to him was just met with an 'Eh?', 'What?' or 'Huh?'

Sometime later I worked on another of his films where a group of us, wearing our own suits, had a hose turned on us. When we complained, all Eric would say was, 'Stop moaning. It's all part of the fun of the business'!

I worked a lot with Kenny Everett on his B.B.C. series, appearing in sketches as his double. He could be a strange one. Sometimes he was very agreeable and chatty and on other occasions he would not even say 'Hello'. When the press made it public knowledge that he was gay, he seemed to wear it as a badge. In one sketch I had to come mincing on as a raving, effeminate trollop. I was made up with eye shadow, lipstick, handbag...the lot. In the dressing room he looked at me and asked if I was gay.

'Not really,' I grinned, making light of it, 'I just help them out when they're busy.'

It was an old gag, a stock answer, but it struck me instantly that here was one subject which made him lose his sense of humour. 'No,' he persisted grimly, 'I mean are you really gay?'

I found the question unsettling, mumbled a negative answer and made myself scarce. It put me in mind of another situation I found myself in when I was told I would be appearing in a 'gay bar' scene. I thought this would just involve a bunch of guys sitting around with drinks but when I saw the costume that wardrobe had laid on for me I nearly flipped. Mini skirt, stockings, suspenders, high heels, Dolly Parton wig...! Bearing in mind that the catering bus was parked outside and I would be spending much of my off duty time hanging about on a busy London street, I refused to put it on. This caused a big row with more accusations of being 'unprofessional' but I was adamant. I felt that this was taking one liberty too far.

It's typical of the attitude that very often noddies are not even granted the courtesy of being told what is required of them so that they can make the choice whether they wish to do it or not. Noddies are not expected to possess any dignity and should just be grateful that they are being employed. It happened to me when I was booked to appear on AUNTIE'S ALL TIME GREATS, a celebration of 60 years of B.B.C. television. All I had been told was that they needed me for a lookalike back view. The studio audience was packed with just about every celebrity name you can think of, all in evening dress, and I was kitted out in a terrible 1970's shirt and tank top. The set up was too complicated to warrant a full explanation, but I was required to walk on behind the presenters, Frank Skinner and David Baddiel, simulate urinating up the back of their sofa and walk off again. During rehearsals I had a feeling this 'joke' was doomed to fail, and sure enough, it fell as flat as a hedgehog crossing the freeway. I walked off to the sound of my own footsteps, the eyes of the nation's cream performers boring malevolently into my back. It was one of the worst moments of my career. Mercifully, when the show was transmitted, my part had been edited out so I was spared my humiliation going public.

Cannon and Ball were agreeable enough, but when I worked on their show with my then duo partner, Graham, it seemed they did not like to be reminded of when they worked the clubs in the early 70's as a musical act. Graham worked the same circuit and often saw them paid off. Mind you, so was Graham. It's happened to us all.

It has been interesting to observe the change in the fortunes of Paul Hogan. I worked on the first Foster's commercial he did in the U.K.. Nobody knew who he was; in fact we all thought he was an extra. Years later, after CROCODILE DUNDEE, we went to Deal in Kent to film another episode of the lager saga. This time things were very different. A whole area around the beach was cordoned off and patrolled by minders in readiness for his arival. When he eventually turned up in a gleaming limo, he spent most of the day inside a luxury trailer while his stand-in took his place for everything save the actual commitment of image to celluloid.

I have done one or two things with John Cleese, usually for Video Arts, the training film company he used to own, and thought him a little stand-offish. However, he did endear himself to a bunch of extras on one production when he was sitting within earshot of their discussion on labotomies.

'Look,' he put in, very seriously, 'if anyone tried to give me a labotomy, I would give them a piece of my mind!'

I will add that when another aquaintance of mine was worked mercilessly on one of Cleese's films, was given dialogue and even made to perform a stunt, he was told by Cleese, having quite rightly asked for more money, that he should not get ideas above his station!

Other actors and actresses who I have personally seen to demonstrate bad attitudes have included Oliver Tobias, Ian Charleson, Hywel Bennett, Lysette Anthony, Joan Collins and Jill Gasgoigne. Johnny Rotten would probably take a perverse delight in inclusion in this list as he goes to such lengths to live up to his image. Suffice to say that he surprised no one by acting like a slob on TOP OF THE POPS. The female half of DEMPSEY AND MAKEPEACE, Glynis Barbour, wouldn't win any awards for courtesy either. I had to appear in a scene with her where we had to squash quite closely together. She made it obvious that she found my presence totally distasteful, trying desperately to ignore me save for the pained look on her hard, haughty face, as if something foul had died beneath her nostrils. To be honest, I wasn't over keen on standing in the pockets of this ice maiden myself.

Much as I love FOOLS AND HORSES, I can't say I was over impressed by the behaviour of Nicholas Lyndhurst. He seemed anti-extra from the very start of my stint on the programme. He also appeared to have a problem with his public, many of whom naturally enough congregated wherever we were filming, and he particularly objected to domestic cameras. I never saw him give an autograph with good grace. Having said that, others have told me that he is very nice to work with, so nothing is cut and dried. As I say, it's all down to personal perception and circumstance.

By contrast, David Jason was great and played up to his 'Del Boy' image, much to the delight of the passing populace. And why not? It didn't take much effort and served to enhance his popularity.

I once heard a wonderful retort from that busiest of actors, the late Denholm Elliott. (He really did seem to be in everything.) A small group of us were on a commercial with him and were all lumped together to relax in the same Winnebago. Mr. Elliott sat at the far end reading a newspaper whilst the noddies, out of boredom, were indulging in a political discussion.

'Did you know,' exclaimed some wag, 'that if Labour get in, no one will be permitted by law to earn more than twenty five thousand a year?'

The wonderful actor looked up over his paper. 'Twenty five thousand?' he mused, softly, 'Why, some people earn that in a day.'

Amidst very tight security, I have filmed on the doorstep of 10 Downing Street, but I'm afraid I have no juicy gossip involving the Prime Minister. The nearest I got to that was when my brother and I, dressed as 1930's working types, were doing some filming at a location near the Elephant and Castle. On the face of it, this area is not very savoury, but we noticed that we were close to a little haven of repectability where the buildings were cleaner and there was no sign of garbage or dog faeces. As we huddled on a corner in flat hats and braces, a familiar looking figure lumbered up the street towards us, eyebrows wafting in the breeze.

'Hey look,' I chuckled, 'It's Dennis Healey.'

I was joking, but, strangely enough, it really was him.

'Hello,' he said, confirming by his voice that he could be no one else, 'what's going on here then? Benny Hill?'

He gestured towards a fellow extra who bore a passing resemblance to the said comedian. I told him he was mistaken and that we were making a heavy drama.

'What a pity. I love Benny Hill. What is it then...the dole queue? Haw! Haw! Thank the Tories for that, eh? Haw! Haw!'

And away he went. It seems he lived just around the corner.

It puts me in mind of when brother Ray and I were guests at the Water Rat's Ball many moons ago, when Harold Wilson, the then Prime Minister, was guest of honour. We were seated just below the top table where Harold embarked on a speech of seemingly un-ending tedium. This coupled with the fact that Ray had only that morning returned from a trip to Australia, my brother was sent into his very own form of political protest. Much to my amusement, and not a little embarrassment, Ray, suffering from jet lag, slumped back in his seat fast asleep!

To me, one of life's greatest crimes was the meteoric rise to fame of a certain teenaged page three bimbo. Why this very ordinary little girl, whose only claim to stardom apparently rested on her oversized mammaries, should have been elevated to such giddy heights was beyond me. I believe the public were victims of a massive con trick and were hypnotised, by blanket media coverage, into believing that this girl really had talent. I became infuriated at the constant sight of her zeppelin-like tits being thrust at me from the pages of virtually every journal I happened to open, and of being told that she was every man's favourite woman. She certainly wasn't mine. I remember one dunder-headed interview where she was quoted as saying that fame hadn't changed her (yawn!); she still liked fried egg sandwiches! Jesus! I'm sure she grew to believe her own publicity.

I base this on my own sight of her when we filmed a Sun commercial outside the Odeon , Leicester Square, one night. En masse, we had to push, shove and clamour to get near her with soppy cries, as she stepped out of a car dressed in sequins and furs. Her father, who was, I believe, also her manager, was there in force with her minder, both of them taking themselves very seriously as they warned us all to keep our distance. The absurdity of the event stuck in my craw as I took in this tableau of grown extras, many of whom had more talent in their toe nail clippings than the 'star' had in her entire body, making idiots of themselves at the feet of this chubby little painted creature. I simply could not bring myself to co-operate and had to walk away.

Her minder, I am told, did a bit of film extra work himself and made the mistake of objecting when a couple of professional jibbers pushed in front of him in a paying out queue. In no uncertain terms, they told him where to go.

'Do you know who I am?' he queried, preening his muscles. When he told them, he was met with howls of derision. Following this up with a warning that he was a martial arts expert, he was then knocked to the ground by a single punch!

Grace Jones is not really one of my favourite people but I will grant her top marks for style. Love her or loathe her, she is a most striking woman as was emphasised during the making of one of the James Bond films. We were shooting a big horse racing scene at Ascot involving a crowd of some four or five hundred extras. When lunch was called, we had to make our way across a busy main road to the food. This was proving to be no easy task what with a stream of never ending speeding vehicles, until Ms. Jones turned up. Nothing was going to stop her from crossing the road. Looking like she had been chiselled out of polished black onyx and dressed from head to toe in flowing, scarlet robes, she strode straight into the traffic and stood with her long legs astride, arms spread defiantly like Moses parting the waves. Cars and trucks screeched to a halt on every side, doubtless struck senseless by this vision. I am amazed that there wasn't a multi pile up, but she got us our lunch!

Rowan Atkinson and Rik Mayall were both un-assuming chaps in spite of their fearsome public images pertaining to the characters they play. I remember Rowan, dressed as Boedicea, falling out of his chariot amongst a mob of us playing Roman soldiers. As the good natured laughter rocked around him, he was actually blushing and lost for words. He struck me as almost shy, unlike Mel Smith who made himself many non-speaking enemies when he uttered vitriolic remarks about extras on a chat show.

Peter Bowles has a reputation for being difficult to work with and is very pernickety about details before he shoots a scene. Arguably, this could be excused as professionalism. The Two Ronnies were also a bit like that.

And now, confession time...sort of! Once, during the filming of a costume ball, the crowd were told to 'live it up', ya-hooing, leaping in the air, throwing streamers and whatever else was to hand. A famous, very classy actress was to make her entrance down a flight of majestic stairs, but the take was ruined by a hard, stale bread roll which struck her full in the face. She screamed and staggered, clutching her pretty, flattened nose. The studio was in uproar. 'Who threw that?!' roared the floor manager as I made myself scarce, nipping sheepishly behind the cyclerama. Yes, I was the guilty one. It was an accident, of course, but I guess I should have been a little more discerning with my aim. I remember that moment of slow motion, shock horror as I watched that roll taking it's perfect trajectory towards those beautiful features and helplessly wincing as it struck home. No one saw me, thank God, but it was an awful moment. She recovered soon enough, but I won't name her just in case she happens to hear of this and comes gunning for me!

I think one of the most embarrassing incidents I ever suffered happened during the making of the commercial where I played the infamous walrus. Apart from two other characters in skins, one as the hare and the other as the dormouse, all the other principals were well known. The shoot lasted four days during which time we were ferried out to a big department store in Luton. The hare was played by a dancer named Phil, who was an amiable fellow, while the dormouse was played by a poisonous little bastard who I shall call Ricky. I soon sussed what kind of a person he was. In the dressing room, on the first day, he was very full of himself, boasting and making nasty cracks about various people. Suddenly, he turned to me and very snottily asked if I was his driver. That was just the start of it. Over the next few days he became an almighty pain in the butt, but the clincher came on the final day over lunch.

We three animals had the honour, as featured artistes, to be eating with the principals and we were seated together at a long table with the likes of Windsor Davies, John Inman, June Whitfield, etc.. At our end of the table, Phil, Ricky and I sat across from three disc jockeys; Greg Edwards, Kid Jensen and Tony Blackburn. It was a pleasant enough meal and the assembled company were all getting along nicely. Tony Blackburn was talking about the lack of variety on British radio and how there should be more stations to cater for different tastes, when, out of the blue, Ricky spoke up... 'Oh yes, you say that, Blackburn, but you just like to hear the sound of your own voice.'

The table was stunned into silence. Phil and I looked at each other in despair as Ricky rambled on. He was slightly drunk, which didn't help.

'Don't you realise how unpopular you are, Blackburn? No one can stand you. You just want to brainwash the nation...' and so on. It was real squirm making stuff. Poor Tony, having recovered from the initial blow, sought to defend himself.

'What are you talking about? I was just saying there should be more choice on the radio...'

'You don't mean it. You talk drivel, like on your show. Why don't you just die a death...'

Like the Cherie Lunghi incident, I wanted the floor to open and swallow me up. The danger here, once again, was that we animals would be categorised as three of a kind. Greg Edwards tried to light heartedly diffuse the situation but our charming dormouse was really going for it. It all wound down into the most dreadful of atmospheres.

Later that afternoon, Tony Blackburn came into the wardrobe room where Ricky lay curled up on the floor in his costume, sleeping off the effects of his chateau neuf du stroppy. Tony took one look at the prone figure and I could see from his expression that he would have loved to give him a kick.

'Go on,' I urged, 'do it.'

We grinned at each other and he went through the motions of raising his foot. He didn't carry it through, but if he had I don't think a single court in the land would have convicted him.

Ricky's next job, as he vainly told us, was also in a skin. He was off to Cameroon to play a chimpanzee in the forthcoming Tarzan epic GREYSTOKE. I have never seen him since so, if there is any justice, maybe he got swallowed by a boa constrictor.

Finally, a mention here of a couple of extras who made it... kind of. Actually, the only one I know of, from more recent years, who reached the top was Jonathan Ross. He paid his dues as an extra for a while, although I knew his brothers, Miles and Adam, much better than I knew him. His mother, Martha, was a very regular face in the crowd.

Years ago I worked a lot with a burly ex-boxer who was desperate to break out of the noddy world. He was in demand though, and there being lots happening in those days, he was working regularly. Undaunted, he spent his evenings at drama classes. Eventually, in spite of having a family to support, he took a chance and packed up noddy-dom altogether to give his acting career a chance. After an initial struggle, putting on his own plays and self promoting his name, his efforts paid off and he started to get parts. His name is Glen Murphy and he has since co-produced at least one film and plays George, one of the main characters in LONDON'S BURNING.

A similar tale lies in the success story of Graham Cole, an actor/singer who was well ensconced in the land of Nod before landing a regular part as P.C. Stamp in THE BILL. This role has built up nicely for him over the years and he became one of the leading players.

Glen and Graham are both nice guys who still pass the time of day with their old compatriots in the ranks. Good luck to them.

THE
OLD
TIMER

'WE'LL MEET AGAIN"
(L.W.T.)

**AMERICAN
BOMBER CREW**
Over here, over paid
and over-the-top accents!

In the burning desert wastes of Dorset ....
'THE KENNY EVERETT SHOW" (B.B.C.)

THE FUTURE?

I have by no means painted the whole picture, but I hope I have managed to give a sketchy impression of life as an extra.

It is an unreal way to make a living. Sometimes fun, sometimes hell, it has been financially rewarding (at times), frequently unpredictable, extremely insecure and devoid of merit, and it can guarantee, if one gets bitten by the bug, total obscurity. For anyone nurturing the slightest desire to be discovered, it is a definite no-no. It is very easy to fall into the trap of money to work on film and television sets, but aspiring thespians should always weigh up the blow their budding reputations will receive by becoming a face in the crowd.

There have been exceptions, but so few they hardly count. If one treats it in the right way, never taking it too seriously, then it can serve its purpose. Requirement number one must be a thick skin. Always remember, you can be replaced at the flick of an assistant's walkie-talkie, so you have virtually no bargaining power. It is casual work and should be treated as such. The happiest extras are those with other activities outside of the business.

The game has changed a lot and the rules, regulations and agreements became so complicated that I began to lose touch. Many new agencies opened (some of them run by out of work extras!) but there are only so many slices to the cake. Owing to the general recession, cost cutting and a host of other reasons, work decreased and the business became hopelessly overcrowded, largely with scores of bona fide artistes (who at one time would not be seen dead as an extra) affected by the general slump in showbiz joining the noddy ranks. Also, a worrying tendency began to grow amongst the companies to use ordinary members of the public. At first this could be stopped, but now they have the law on their side, as per this recent quote from a trade journal; '...legislation against restrictive practices and the growth of the independent production sector has created a climate which will allow an increasing number of inexperienced performers to undercut and squeeze out the professionals.'

In other words, thanks to the Tory success in smashing the power of the unions, it is now illegal for anyone to be kept out of a job if they are not a member of a said union. No more closed shop. The political and moral rights and wrongs of this are not to be discussed here, but the effect has been very hard on background artistes. The companies are saying, 'Why pay all this money to Equity and F.A.A. members when we can get crowds from the benefit office who will gladly work for a fraction of the cost?' It is quite common now for open advertisements to be placed in job centres asking for extras. All very well and about time too, some people may be thinking, but the point is that livings have been taken away from those who have been professional noddies for most of their lives. Throwing open the flood gates has surely got to cause aggravation for everyone in the long run. Using amateurs who are completely green when it comes to film making, even when they are only in the crowd, must backfire eventually. People will get sick of all the hanging about, they won't come back for continuity shots, they will stare into the camera, all sorts of things, the result of which has got to be a drop in standards and added problems in crowd control.

Also, the Tory government insisted that the big television companies farm out more of their work to independent producers. This means that one will still be engaged to work for the likes of the B.B.C., but not under the cosy conditions we were once so accustomed to. Now, one could well be sub-contracted to some rag-bag, fly-by-night production company who would not touch an Equity agreement with a ten foot stick. One is paid for the day, of course, but it is just basic money. No Walk-Ons, no repeat fees, as a rule. Within these changes, the official agreements still remain as a guideline, but only as that. The new cut price system became the order of the day. As more corners were cut, less productions were being made. The staging of big, lavish dramas fell noticably, yet they were in abundance at one time. I used to spend half my life at the B.B.C. Television Centre dressed in funny gowns and wigs, but, owing to costs, these expensive productions have been largely replaced by the purchase of American and Australian imports. Many of the shows made in Britain now seem to be of the 'game show' variety. Cheap television, you see.

One of the most dramatic changes came with a string of circumstances which shattered the sub-structure of Central Casting. For decades, this organisation had total control over all the film extra work in the United Kingdom and it seemed unthinkable that things would ever be any different. However, first of all there were a series of alterations made between the F.A.A. and P.A.C.T. regarding pay and working conditions. After years of solidarity, there seemed to be a general slide in favour of the producers, gradually eroding many of the perks that had been built up over a long time. Categories and special payments grew more difficult to attain, then we lost the right to payment in cash on the day. This caused uproar in the F.A.A. rank and file, but, given time, cheque payments within ten days were begrudgingly accepted. And then the unbelievable happened. One of the Central Casting office employees, obviously spotting the potential, broke away and formed a rival agency called 'Atmos'. Everyone said she was bound to fail but she went from strength to strength and was soon taking much of the film work that would previously have gone automatically to Casting. Incredibly, within a year, Casting was in big trouble and this rival woman actually returned and took it over, forming an amalgamation called Atmos Central Casting. You had to hand it to her for sheer enterprise! She charged everyone a 'registration fee' of £25 to come back into the fold. More resentment, but there was no shortage of people, including me, who paid up. What choice did we have? At the time it seemed that she had us over a barrel.

Now a real hornet's nest had been stirred up. Disillusioned, one of the oldest hands in the Casting office left and formed his own agency which he called Ex-Casting! Confusing or what? The noddies did not know which way to turn. With union powers smashed, the F.A.A. couldn't help us. We were left floundering in the dark, wondering which faction to side with. Having never worked for Atmos, I decided to go with the devil I knew and joined Ex-Casting. He gave me a job on the day I registered and over the next three years he employed me twice more!

In the meantime, the F.A.A., which most of us had given up on, found itself a new General Secretary who immediately seemed like a breath of fresh air in the industry. Fighting against apparently impossible odds, he set about creating a refreshing new climate. Instead of the 'hands up' attitude that had permeated of late, he questioned everything and started court cases all over the place. The F.A.A. and Atmos C.C. became mortal enemies. Then (this is beginning to read like a film plot itself!) Atmos C.C. went bust owing artistes thousands in unpaid fees.

Well, where did that leave we poor noddies who only wanted to earn a living? The answer is 'up the creek'! Film work, such as it was by this time, (there was a record bad year in British based film production) went to the agents. The F.A.A. agreed fees were now subject to commission thus making us worse off than we had ever been. On top of this, the companies, making the most of the situation and knowing we were all desperate, started to offer deals. For example, a flat fee for a twelve hour day (which initially meant thirteen hours as they no longer counted lunch) or even worse. Each deal that was accepted seemed to get topped by a tighter one. Where would it all end, we wondered? Were we to end up paying the producers for the honour of working for them?

A new Equity agreement sold us down the river too. With the I.T.V. companies, our representatives negotiated away our expenses and achieved a 20% cut in our earnings for any calls which included more than forty one people. (I hear this was later revoked by popular demand.) The B.B.C. did away with it's Walk-On 2 and the category became a blanket Walk-On, covering everything for a few quid more. I went on one job where they unexpectedly (even though I had earned it) endorsed my pay chit for a maximum special action payment, but they changed their minds and by the time I received the cheque it had been deducted. I couldn't understand how they could do this. Surely, the chit, signed and agreed by the artiste and the authorised assistant, was a legally binding document, otherwise what was the point of having it? I felt there was a case for the small claims court, but, of course, no one dares to do it for fear of jeopardising future work.

All sorts of things began to happen; new controversies daily. Stories of midnight raids on offices, lock outs, litigation and the new F.A.A. General Secretary being thrown out on his ear for alleged misconduct! I began to distance myself more and more from the whole sorry business. It was all doom and gloom, but fortunately I began to get busier with my other career as a performer and started to lose touch. I was doing increasing amounts of stage work and began to feel more fulfilled as the bookings increased. My main duo partner and I decided to specialise in promoting our own themed act which took off rather well as we prostituted our talents around the countryside in various guises as cowboys, hillbillies, tudor minstrels, Irish buskers, pirates or whatever was required. Occasionally, we appeared in concert or worked as a band, releasing a recorded product of our own material which was well received. In tandem with this, I went back to performing as a solo act, eventually plunging myself into my first summer season for years when I was contracted as a principal artiste in a Wild West revue show in Wales. How refreshing it was to get away from the noddy scene for weeks on end.

In general, long periods began to go by when I started to realise that I wasn't taking any extra work and, better still, wasn't missing it. That's not to say that I could afford to turn it down, but at least I reached a point where I was not wholly dependent upon it. But, such is the volatile nature of this business, my fortunes rise and fall and the need to check in still exists. It's interesting to note how the game has changed. When I work in the crowd now, it's quite rare to meet up with any of the faces I knew from the old days and I often spend my time alone, with the new faction muttering and wondering who I am. But new faces are appearing in droves, so many of them are strangers to each other. I just try to keep my distance and tell myself that I'm not really a part of it anymore. Wrong attitude, perhaps, but that's how I feel.

On the plus side, it seems that the work situation has levelled out now. The F.A.A. has amalgamated with BECTU and the chaos has largely been sorted out. New agreements have been authorised, deals have been outlawed and work actually seems to be picking up again for those who are serious about it, but I'm sure it will never return to the way it was. A whole new breed of extra has taken over with a completely new approach. I guess it was inevitable. (At least the changes have broken the monopoly of the 'barrow boy' fraternity. Tee, hee!)

And the latest danger? Technology! The computer age! Virtual reality graphics are now so advanced (and getting better all the time) there seems to be nothing they cannot potentially achieve on screen. They have already used it on at least one big picture I know of, to simulate a huge baseball crowd. If they can make realistic individual dinosaurs, why not noddies? And then the lead actors... there seems to be no end to it.

So what do I care? I worked through the swansong of the halcyon days of noddydom and now I'd like to think it's time to move on. More than enough of my life has been spent as a smudge in the background. I am doing prestige work these days and I am operating in different circles amidst people who associate with me for my abilities. Who needs noddying?

Still, next week looks a bit bleak... hmmm... could do with a job or two... Funny how as you grow older you notice your category changing. I don't get those disco or soldier jobs anymore... anyway, I'm not getting my hair cut... unless the price is right, of course... perhaps I'd better just check in...

'Hello, it's Mi...'

'Nothing at the moment.'

Click. Brrrrrrr...

EXAMPLES OF FILM TERMINOLOGY

'Check the gate': At the end of a series of 'takes', the gate (the camera area directly between the lens and the unexposed film) must be scrutinised to ensure that no obstructions have marred the image.

'Hair in the gate': Expression used to describe any foreign body found in the gate, but it can literally refer to a 'hair', which on screen would appear as a giant tram line.

'That's a wrap!': End of the day (or night's) shooting schedule.

'Put down some Grouchos': As in Groucho Marx .... Marks ... pieces of tape placed on the floor to mark an actor's position.

'Turn over': Instruction to start the camera motor.

'Speed': Camera running up to required speed.

'Action': Instruction to artistes to commence acting. 'Background action' is for movement in general.

'Cut': Stop the take.

'Give it the Spanish Archer': Derivation of 'El-Bow'. To 'give it the elbow' .. get rid of.

'Max': Max Factor ... Actor

'Number ones, please': Take up original positions.

'Honey Wagon': Mobile location toilet. Origin of the expression? Your guess is as good as mine, but I've heard some revolting theories!

'Red light and bell!': Flashing red light and ringing bell in studio which warns of impending take.

'Brutes, Pups and Bashers': Different types of lights.

'Rushes': First viewing of the day's takes.

'One more!': Means at least three more takes.

'Wild track': Atmospheric sound recordings.

'Final checks!': Nothing to do with your fee!

ODE TO AN EXTRA

Ned was a full time extra,
A face in the mob, that was all...
But a face seldom seen
On the wide silver screen,
More likely a blur by the wall.

He wanted to be a film hero,
Fighting villains and getting girl's glances,
But all that he got
Was his face out of shot
And a lifetime of thrown away chances.

His mother had sent him to stage school,
He toured as an actor, so proud...
Yet fame passed him by
Though he really did try
To do more than blend into the crowd.

Auditions were getting him nowhere,
He became an anonymous noddy...
No longer to speak,
He felt like a freak
As he hired out his de-focussed body.

The side of his head was in ZULU,
His shape was in CARRY ON JACK,
His ear starred with Fonda,
He drove by on a Honda
And in ALFIE you just saw his back.

He was once directed by Hitchcock,
The great man said 'Out of my way!'
He once spilled his dinner
In the lap of Mike Winner
Inspiring a DEATH WISH that day.

His T.V. career began slowly,
Showing up in the Beeb's MANOR BORN..
With Rolf he stroked spaniels,
Disappeared by Paul Daniels
But nobody noticed he'd gone.

As a Dalek he showed great emotion,
In EASTENDERS he walked out the door...
He once had a line
In that show SUMMER WINE
But it stayed on the cutting room floor.

As the years went by he grew older,
His face became craggy and pitted...
In WAITING FOR GOD
They said 'Poor old sod'
And assumed he was surely half witted.

A career of great promise was over
He died as he queued for his tea...
But they held up the hearse
For the crew must go first,
As they mumbled 'Who the hell's he?'

And so he ascended to glory...
To that Heavenly set in the clouds...
At God's right hand side
He stands there with pride,
He's the angel who's lost in the crowd!

Mike Martin

139

APPENDAGE

Just for posterity, there follows an (almost) complete breakdown of the work relevant to this book done by the author between 1979 and 1997. 'OTHER' denotes promotional, photographic engagements or training/public information films.

1979: TELEVISION: Top of the Pops, Shoestring, Goodbye Darling, That Crazy Woman, Shelley, The Onedin Line, King Arthur, Juke Box Jury, Armchair Thriller, Secret Army, Dreams of Leaving, Grundy, Murder Rap, Breakaway, Kate the Good Neighbour, The Professionals, George and Mildred, Piggy in the Middle, The Generation Game, Penmarric, Family Fortunes, London Night Out, The Mike Yarwood Show, To the Manor Born.
FILMS: The Birth of the Beatles, Rough Cut, Breaking Glass.
COMMERCIALS: Tennent's Lager, Molson's Lager, United Biscuits, Carb'n Off, I.D.D. Post Office, Washing Machines.
OTHER: What is Profit?, Polymedia.

1980: TELEVISION: Fancy Wanders, Cold Feet, The Gentle Touch, Speak for Yourself, Armchair Thriller, Hamlet, Arrivals 1 & 2, Cover, Citizen Smith, Born and Bred, Watch All Night, Shoestring, Top of the Pops, Tale of Two Cities, Something in Disguise, The Dick Emery Show, Great Preachers, The Lena Zavaroni Show, Nelson, Closing Ranks, Oppenheimer, Keats, Contract, Mackenzie, To Serve Them All My Days, Going Gently, The Professionals, Standing in for Henry, Just Liz, The Morecambe and Wise Show, If You Go Down to the Woods Today..., Angels, Bognor, Passmore, Wolcott, Elizabeth Alone, The Screamers, The Other Arf, The Generation Game, Seconds Out, The Incredible Mr. Tanner, The Borgias, The Union, Sink or Swim, Closing Ranks, Diamonds, The Jim Davidson Show, A Fine Romance, The Chinese Detective, Virginia Fly is Drowning, West End Tales, The Basil Brush Christmas Show, Over the Moon,The Brack Report, Yes Minister, Nanny, Piggy in the Middle. FILMS: Dick Turpin, Eye of the Needle, Tale of Two Cities.
COMMERCIALS: Carling Black Label, Worthington E, T.W.A., M.F.I., Tartan Bitter. OTHER: Anti Drink Drive.

1981: TELEVISION: Maybury, When the Boat Comes In, The Union, Robin's Nest, The Borgias, Top of the Pops, Timon of Athens, Baby Talk, Nationwide, Blake's Seven, Till Death Us Do Part, Thriller, The Box Wallah, Sorry, The Story of Ruth, Love Story, Never the Twain, Bognor, Diamonds, Minder, The Day of the Triffids, Are You Being Served?, Tom, Dick and Harriet, We'll Meet Again, Terry and June, Passing Through, Badger by Owl Light, The Treasure Seekers, Shine On Harvey Moon, World's End, Bergerac, Four In A Million, Sink or Swim, A Voyage Round My Father, No Visible Scar, Going to Work, Nancy Astor, Fame is the Spur, The Critic, Spooner's Patch, Life After Death, Starstruck, B.B.C. Training Exercises, Now and Then, Seconds Out, London is Drowning, Nicholas Nickleby, Dr. Who, Bird of Prey, The Gentle Touch, County Hall, On the Line, Gulliver's Travels, Alexa, Friday Night and Saturday Morning, Triangle, Pictures, Mitch, The Jim Davidson Show, Henry V1, Murphy's Mob. FILMS: Churchill, Brittania Hospital, Oliver Twist. COMMERCIALS: M.F.I., Premium Bonds, Winterman Cigars, Carling Lager, Benson and Hedges, Impulse, Berni Inns, British Rail, Hofmeister, Foster's, Barbican, Stone's Bitter, KP Peanuts, Daily Express Bingo. OTHER: Bols, Asthma Prevention.

1982: TELEVISION: Mitch, The Kenny Everett Show, Sorry I'm a Stranger Here Myself, Radio, Holding the Fort, Jane in Search of a Job, Wayne and Albert, Easter 2016, After the Party, The Other Arf, Young at Heart, Agatha, King Lear, Take Three Women, Depression, Shine on Harvey Moon, A Gifted Adult, Fairground, John David, Beatrix Potter, Q10, Another Flip for Dominic, The Chinese Detective, B.B.C. Camera Training, Shackleton, The Rowan Atkinson Show, Wembley Conference, Cannon and Ball Show, Jackanory Playhouse, The Dick Emery Show, Black Adder, Squadron, Making Good, The Stanley Baxter Show, Grand Duo, Falkland's War Tribute, The Kelly Monteith Show, Cymbeline, Partners, Captain's Doll, The Mike Yarwood Show, Hard Word, Now and Then, Tucker's Luck, Old Men at the Zoo, The Boy Who Won the Pools, Cuffy, Chance in a Million, Metal Mickey, Family Fortunes, Yes Minister, The Climber, A Married Man, Jemima Shaw. FILMS: Who Dares Wins, Walter, The Nation's Health, Octopussy, Ploughman's Lunch. COMMERCIALS: Northern Bank, Ford, John Smith's Lager,

Post Office, Carling Black Label, McEwan's Lager, McVities, Telephone Directory, Branston's Pickle, British Airways, Hansa Lager, Woolworths, Allied Carpets, Guinness, Watneys, Hertz.
OTHER: Milk, B.M.W., Barclay's Bank, Lloyd's Bank, Simpson's Clothes.

1983: TELEVISION: The Kenny Everett Show, No Problem, Strangers and Brothers, Give Us A Break, Murphy's Mob, The Morecambe and Wise Show, Auf Wiedersehn Pet, The Chas and Dave Show, Jury, Stan's Last Game, Rumpole of the Bailey, They Came From Somewhere Else, Gathering Seed, Desert of Lies, The Keith Harris Show, The Brief, Going to Work, By The Sword Divided, The Gentle Touch, Pericles, Diana, Witches and the Grinnygog, Minder, Storyboard, The Case of the Frightened Lady, Missing From Home, The Lady is a Tramp, Doctor Who, Amy, Souvenir, It Takes a Worried Man, The Little and Large Show, Tucker's Luck, The Kit Curran Radio Show, Hollywood or Bust. FILMS: Lassiter, Charlie, The Zany Adventures of Robin Hood, Master of the Game, The First Olympics, Squaring the Circle, Czechmate, Electric Dreams, Lace.
COMMERCIALS: Bass, John Smith's, Woolworths, Carling, Wilson's Bitter, L.E.B., Brittania Building Society, London Transport, Tartan Bitter, Kestrel Lager, McEwan's, Twix, Fortune, Ford, Peugot, Persil, Decor 8, Tennents, Harvey's Finesse, British Rail, American Express, Dixon's, Daddy's Sauce, Findus, Trophy Bitter.
OTHER: Ford, London Transport, British Airways, Anti Drink.

1984: TELEVISION: Knees Up, Blue Money, Blood Royal, Winter Sunlight, Chance in a Million, Profile of Arthur Mason, What's My Line?, Dramarama, Mr. Palfrey, Rachel and Rosie, The Optimists, The Lenny Henry Show, Oxbridge Blues, Dempsey and Makepeace, Lytton's Diary, Late Starter, Occupation Democrats, Big Deal, Fraggle Rock, Me and My Girl, The Kelly Monteith Show, Secret Servant, By the Sword Divided, Magnox, Bulman, Comrade Dad, Bomber Pilot, The Bill, The Mistress, The Little and Large Show, Ever Decreasing Circles, Dutch Girls, The Two Ronnies, The Laughter Show, Yes Minister, Hilary, The Benny Hill Show, Magnox, Last of the Summer Wine. FILMS: Success is the Best Revenge, 1984, Paint Me a Murder, Ellis Island, Space Vampires, The Bride, A View to a Kill, Jenny's

War, S.S., The Dirty Dozen's Next Mission.
COMMERCIALS: Webster's Bitter, Guinness, Polaroid, Cadbury's,
Tartan Bitter, British Rail, Findus, Ansell's Bitter, Escapade, Allied
Carpets, McEwan's, DHL, Jacob's Crackers, Omega Watches,
Schreiber, Grindlay's Bank, Panama Cigars, Apple Computers,
Tennents, Harp Lager. OTHER: Crouzet, Dunhill Cigarettes, Anti
Smoking, American Express, Solid Fuel Advisory Service, Woolworths,
British Aerospace, Wimpey Homes.

1985: TELEVISION: Eastenders, Who's Baby?, Mr. Palfrey, Cat's Eyes,
Tripods, What's My Line?, The Kenny Everett Show, Adrian Mole,
The Keith Harris Show, Hold the Back Page, The Mike Yarwood Show,
Grange Hill, The Bill, Magnum, The Lenny Henry Show, Dempsey and
Makepeace, To Have and to Hold, Caucasian Chalk Circle, Remington
Steele, Bergerac, No Place Like Home, In Sickness and in Health, Big
Deal, King of the Ghetto, Comrade Dad, Running Scared, Bluebell,
Oedipus the King, Strike it Lucky, Lytton's Diary, Hot Metal, First
Among Equals, Watching, Slip Up. FILMS: Deceptions, 55 Lime
Street, Thirteen to Dinner, Prospects, Defence of the Realm, Paradise
Postponed, Room with a View, Strong Medicine, Mona Lisa, If
Tomorrow Comes, The Whistle Blower, Whoops Apocalypse, Little
Shop of Horrors. COMMERCIALS: Lowenbrau, Toby Bitter, Pizza
Hut, Ricoh Video, Nationwide, Foster's, After Eight Mints, Pizzaland,
Olympus Cameras, Fine Fare, TSB, Delmonte, Faust Lager, Turkish
Bank, James Last Album, Shell, Phillips, Sainsburys, Heinz, Guinness,
Central Office of Information, French Connection, Findus, Anadin.
OTHER: Sweet Bird of Youth, Transaif, Safeways, Hotel Brochure,
Midland Bank, British Telecom, Big Audio Dynamite Pop Video,
Computers.

1986: TELEVISION: Drummonds, Dempsey and Makepeace, The
Singing Detective, Ladies in Charge, First Among Equals, Boogie
Outlaws, Pass the Buck, Ever Decreasing Circles, King and Castle,
Call Me Mister, The Little Princess, The Kenny Everett Show, Only
Fools and Horses, Cat's Eyes, Executive Stress, Chocky, Pink-Putter
and Sweet, Big Deal, Cuckoo's Sister, Full House, Strike it Rich,
London's Burning, The Growing Pains of Adrian Mole, Big George is
Dead, All in Good Faith, Father Matthew's Daughter, Duty Free,

Slinger's Day, Eastenders, Rumpole of the Bailey, Our Geoff. FILMS: Little Shop of Horrors, Little Dorrit, The Fourth Protocol, Intimate Contact, Crazy Like a Fox. COMMERCIALS: The Sun, Texas Home Care, Barclay's Bank, French Bank, Hanson Trust, Texaco, Sun Alliance, TSB, Mail on Sunday, Woolworths, Braumaister Lager, Sunday Express, Milk, Rado Watches, Virgin, Schweppes, Alex, Stella Artois, Lloyd's Bank, Blue Arrow. OTHER: Honda, Ford, IBM.

1987: TELEVISION: Bust, Ffizz, Murder at the Farm, Piggy Bank, B.B.C. Staff Training Exercises, Love in the Afternoon, Tandoori Nights, The Bill, Tickets for the Titanic, The Russ Abbot Show, Eric Sykes Special, Five Alive, Eastenders, Executive Stress, Grange Hill, Radical Chambers, Gems, London Embassy, The Roland Rat Show, The Kenny Everett Show, The Money Men, Campaign, Fiddler's Green, Wish Me Luck, Three Up and Two Down, Pulaski, Hot Metal, Ever Decreasing Circles, Simon and the Witch, Thin Air, Andy Capp, Whatever Next, Tumbledown, London's Burning, Hi De Hi, Fifteen to One, King and Castle. FILMS: The Living Daylights, Easy Money, The Fear, Hawks, The Accidental Tourist, The Fruit Machine, A Very British Coup. COMMERCIALS: The Sun, Kellogs, Lazertag, The Independent, Toby Bitter, Continental Airlines, Hertz, Abbey National, TSB, COI, Australian Finance, British Caledonian, Piedmont Airlines, Lucozade, Hofmeister, Royal Life Insurance, Eagle Star, Kronenbourg, Nefax, BP, British Gas, Rickard, Top Man, Midland Bank, American Express, Fiat, Orbis, Hamlet Cigars. OTHER: Polaroid, Melrose Training, Volkswagen, EEC, Swedish Shares, History of Surgery, British Gas Pensions, Identity Parade.

1988: TELEVISION: Fifteen to One, Home James, The Time the Place, Dogfood Dan and the Carmarthern Cowboy, King and Castle, Don't Wait Up, Casting Off, The Bill, Shake Hands Forever, Colin's Sandwich, Square Deal, Crimewatch File, Streets Apart, Meadows Green, Rumpole, The Manageress, Simon and the Witch, Flying in the Branches, Inspector Morse, Bread, Ffizz, Wish Me Luck, London's Burning, Continuing Education, The Lenny Henry Show, Bye Bye Baby. FILMS: Duck, Scandal, Dangerous Love, Queen of Hearts, Great Expectations, Monster Maker, Flight 007. COMMERCIALS: Rank Xerox, RVS Insurance, Coca Cola,

Boddington's Bitter, Castella, Fosters, Trophy Bitter, Miller Lite, Tennents, British Steel, Kit Kat, Texas Home Care, Anchor Butter, Krona Margarine, British Airways, Ford. OTHER: British Rail, Halifax Building Society, Ford, Anti Drink Drive, British Airways.

1989: TELEVISION: The Bill, Storyboard, High Street Blues, Only Fools and Horses, Stone Age, Missing Persons, The Paradise Club, Making News, Alas Smith and Jones, Euro Disney Special, Bergerac, Eurocops. FILMS: Killing Dad, The Russia House. COMMERCIALS: Cadburys, Prudential, Scottish Amicable, Seven Up, Fiat, Repsol Oil, Echo, Brittania, Avis, Twiglets, Nat West Bank, Sunday Express, British Telecom, Water Board, Comfort, Carling Black Label, Panache, Amstrad, Tennents, Beefeater Inns, Pampers, Kellogs, Farranti. OTHER: Marriott Hotels, British Airways.

1990: TELEVISION: London's Burning, The Bill, After Henry, The Les Dennis Show, Up the Garden Path, TECX, Birds of a Feather, Waiting for God, The Chronicles of Narnia, Think About Science, Der Kinder, Eastenders, Freddie and Max, The Jasper Carrot Show, On the Up, Rumpole, Bejewelled, Poirrot, The Rita Rudner Show, Noel Edmond's Saturday Roadshow, Inspector Morse, Desmonds, Tell Me That You Love Me, Jeeves and Wooster, The Harry Enfield Show, House of Payne, Only Fools and Horses. FILMS: The Fool, The Paper Man, Shrinks, Robin Hood (Prince of Thieves), Selling Hitler. COMMER-CIALS: The Sun, Barclays, Daily Mail, North West Airlines, MacDonalds, Lloyds, Burger King, Spanish Lottery, British Gas, Crosse and Blackwell, Lunpoly, Heineken, Fairy Liquid, Prudential, Granary Rolls, Cornetto. OTHER: Vauxhall.

1991: TELEVISION: The Bill, Tonight at Eight Thirty, Gone to the Dogs, Doctor at the Top, Love Hurts, On the Up, Les Dennis Laughter Show, Goodbye Cruel World, Rides, The Alexei Sayle Show, The Adventuresome Three, Eastenders, The Piglet Files, A Question of Attribution, Born Kicking, Sam Saturday, Maria's Child, Downtown Lagos. COMMERCIALS: Tennents, Hi-Tec, COI, Irn-Bru, Encore Shampoo, Lucozade. OTHER: London Transport.

1992: TELEVISION: Lobiz, Sam Saturday, Crime Monthly, Clothes in the Wardrobe, Eastenders, Marathon Trailer, Love Hurts, 2.4 Children, The Bill, Between the Lines, The Mushroom Picker, True Crimes, Seconds Out, Grange Hill, Framed, Waiting for God, Statement of Affairs, Ghostwatch, Teenage Health Freak, The Long Road, The Generation Game, Calling the Shots, Second Thoughts, Oasis, The Jasper Carrot Show, Public Eye, Diana (Her True Story). FILMS: The Hour of the Pig, Century. COMMERCIALS: Walker's Crisps, Saga Computers, Beecham's, Radio Rentals, Clerical and Medical, British Telecom. OTHER: Royal Mail, Future Media, Sony.

1993: TELEVISION: The Bill, Us Girls, Wide Eyed and Legless, Frank Stubbs Promotes, Lovejoy, Between the Lines, Hale and Pace, Crime Monthly, K.Y.T.V., The Plant, A Class Act, Newman and Baddiel, Next, Noel's House Party, Sitting Pretty, Chandler and Co., The Knock, Children in Need, Roughnecks, Eastenders. FILM: Four Weddings and a Funeral. COMMERCIALS: Federal Insurance, Argentaria, Do It All, Pert Plus Shampoo, Robinson's, Kraft, Magnum Ice Cream, Cameron's Beer, Daily Mail, Kotex, Hotpoint, Fairy Liquid. OTHER: Air U.K., Nissan, Siemen's Nixdorf, Nat West.

1994: TELEVISION: Chandler and Co., The Bill, Time After Time, The Ten Percenters, Frank Stubbs Promotes, Ellington, Between the Lines, Crime Monthly, Nanny Knows Best, Ghost Hour, Punt and Dennis, Soldier Soldier, Frontiers, Measure for Measure, The Politician's Wife, Down to Earth, Rules of Engagement. FILMS: Scarlett, The Madness of King George, First Knight. COMMERCIALS: U.P.S., Asda, Fuji, Paxo.

1995: TELEVISION: Moving Story, Crown Prosecutor, Chandler and Co., Absence of War, Roughnecks, Karaoke, House of Cards, The Bill, Nelson's Column, Our Friends in the North, Taking Liberties, Ellington, Smith and Jones, Crossing the Border, Soldier Soldier, Fifteen to One, Pie in the Sky. FILMS: Golden Eye, 101 Dalmatians. COMMERCIALS: Rover Cars, Audi, Jet, Asda, B.A.A., The Sun, Health Education Council. OTHER: Thomas Cook.

1996: TELEVISION: The Bill, Silent Witness, Millenium 2, Soldier Soldier, Holding On, The Moonstone, Crime Traveller, Bliss, Auntie's All Time Greats, Sharpe, Broker's Man, Metro Land, Never Mind the Buzzcocks, The Generation Game. FILMS: Firelight, Fever Pitch, Kangaroo Palace, The Saint, Oscar Wilde. COMMERCIALS: I.C.L., Coca Cola, Nat West, Nissan, Nortel. OTHER: British Airways.

1997: TELEVISION: Bramwell, Disney Club, Trauma, Woman In White, Blooming Marvellous, Berkeley Square, Silent Witness, Thieftakers, Christmas Vacation '97.
COMMERCIALS: Nissan, Umbro, British Telecom, Great Western Railway, Persil. FILM: Tomorrow Never Dies.